"Amanda Owen takes on a big probl[...] and receiving what they want. Wom[...] endlessly generous, thoughtful, and self-sacrificing. *Born to Receive* teaches us that women need to complement these skills with those of receiving, of learning how to ask for and accept what we want. Using wit, anecdotes, exercises, and helpful insights, she turns this task into one that is manageable and promises to be very helpful. Owen makes the convincing case that wholeness comes from the joint activity of giving and receiving. Women are experts at giving, but can surely use the help she offers to become equally expert at receiving."

—ROSALIND C. BARNETT, PH.D., co-author of *The New Soft War on Women: How the Myth of Female Ascendance Is Hurting Women, Men—and the Economy*, and senior scientist at Women's Studies Research Center, Brandeis University

"*Born to Receive* is the missing half of the equation that equals flourishing health. This book gives you the steps to becoming a healthy, happy receiver!"

—CHRISTIANE NORTHRUP, M.D., ob/gyn physician and author of the *New York Times* bestsellers *Women's Bodies, Women's Wisdom* and *The Wisdom of Menopause*

"Women have finely tuned the art of giving—now it's time to learn how to receive with grace and gratitude. The practical tools and tips contained in *Born to Receive* will help you to develop the critical skills needed to transition from simply surviving to joyfully thriving."

—LOIS P. FRANKEL, PH.D., author of *Nice Girls Don't Get the Corner Office*

"When you want to take on the life of your dreams, you will want to know how to 'receive' help. *Born to Receive* is a practical guide for women to lean in to superpowers that don't involve grabbing and forcing. Through clear insights and techniques, Amanda Owen shows us how to actively engage our right to receive and specific ways to start opening the floodgates."

—TAMA KIEVES, bestselling author of *This Time I Dance! Creating the Work You Love* and *Inspired & Unstoppable: Wildly Succeeding in Your Life's Work!*, TamaKieves.com

"*Born to Receive* is a must-read for anyone who believes that receiving is taking, or selfish—and consequently feels depleted, unbalanced, or resentful. Amanda Owen has done an amazing job of exploring why we need and deserve to get more out of life, and how to do it."

—LORI DESCHENE, founder of tinybuddha.com and author of *Tiny Buddha's Guide to Loving Yourself*

# Born to Receive

# Born to Receive

~~~~~~~~~~~~~~~~

{ **SEVEN POWERFUL STEPS**
Women Can Take Today to Reclaim
Their Half of the Universe }

## Amanda Owen

TARCHER/PENGUIN
a member of Penguin Group (USA)
New York

JEREMY P. TARCHER/PENGUIN
Published by the Penguin Group
Penguin Group (USA) LLC
375 Hudson Street
New York, New York 10014

USA · Canada · UK · Ireland · Australia
New Zealand · India · South Africa · China

penguin.com
A Penguin Random House Company

Most Tarcher/Penguin books are available at special quantity discounts for bulk
purchase for sales promotions, premiums, fund-raising, and educational needs.
Special books or book excerpts also can be created to fit specific needs.
For details, write: Special.Markets@us.penguingroup.com.

Library of Congress Cataloging-in-Publication Data

Owen, Amanda.
Born to receive : seven powerful steps women can take today to reclaim
their half of the universe / Amanda Owen.
p.       cm.
ISBN 978-0-399-16378-4
1. Need (Psychology).    2. Goal (Psychology).    3. Self-realization in women.
4. Women—Psychology.    I. Title.
BF503.093        2014                2013037686
158.1082—dc23

Printed in the United States of America
1   3   5   7   9   10   8   6   4   2

BOOK DESIGN BY EMILY S. HERRICK

# { Contents }

*Introduction*  ix

**PART ONE.** YOU WERE BORN TO RECEIVE

The Language of Receiving  *3*

What Are Receptivities?  *10*

The ABCs of Receiving  *17*

The Top Ten Features of Skilled Receivers  *20*

What Is Receptive Power?  *21*

The CULTure of Self-Esteem  *25*

**PART TWO.** SEVEN STEPS TO RECLAIM
YOUR HALF OF THE UNIVERSE

**Step One:**
Pay Attention to Your Feelings and Trust Your Intuition  *33*

**Step Two:**
Know What You Want  *56*

**Step Three:**
Ask for Help If You Need It and Accept It
When It's Offered   *78*

**Step Four:**
Be Grateful and Say Thank You   *103*

**Step Five:**
Create Full Reciprocity in Your Relationships   *127*

**Step Six:**
Don't Put Yourself Last or *You* Won't Last   *154*

**Step Seven:**
Be Respectful of Your Past, Have a Vision for Your Future,
but Live in the Moment   *186*

The Past, Future, and Present of Each Step   *201*

*A Summary of the Receive Exercises*   *209*

*A List of Receptivities*   *217*

*Acknowledgments*   *221*

*Resources for Additional Support and Inspiration*   *223*

# { Introduction }

While it takes only a village to raise a child, it seems to take an entire industry of self-help books, retreats, workshops, seminars, spas, life coaches, and counselors to raise the self-esteem of a woman. Too many of us are emotionally fragile and excessively focused on our weight, appearance, and self-esteem. This causes us to be overly dependent on the approval of others, which in turn fuels a frenetic, multitasking lifestyle. And even though we know that stress, unhealthy habits, and preoccupation with our self-esteem and appearance are not helping us, we are not changing. Why?

Our quest for a balanced life collides with a culture that has convinced us that doing for others and pleasing them is more important than paying attention to our own needs. Add to this the prevailing cultural paradigm that encourages competition—a way of life that does not generally appeal to women, as we tend to be more inclusive in our thinking and more relational in our activities.

So, how are we to become whole, balanced individuals when so many of our efforts are directed toward other people, and our social environment champions an "us versus them" mentality? Yes, we want people to consider our needs. But that doesn't mean that we want to trade places and put our feet up, and have everybody cater to our whims. (Although in our most exhausted moments, this seems quite appealing!) What we want is equality.

Although we live in a world where activity, competitiveness, and physical strength are kings, a woman is a queen with her own power. We are half of creation and have governance of the 50 percent that belongs to us—feminine power, receptive power. But with few role models and little information about our natural state, we are vulnerable to messages that tell us we should do more and give more (and eat less).

It is activity and receptivity *together* that create wholeness in oneself and in the world. The path to a balanced life is not reached by endlessly examining our emotions or by filling our days with activities.

My book *The Power of Receiving: A Revolutionary Approach to Giving Yourself the Life You Want and Deserve* provided a foundation and basic tools for living a receptive life. Since its release in 2011, I've heard from people all over the world and from all walks of life, thanking me for giving them a language and a framework for creating a balanced life. Learning about the power of receiving has helped them to be stronger, steadier, happier, and healthier.

I wrote *Born to Receive* to give you new ideas and a radically different approach to achieving your goals, reducing stress, and creating better health and greater happiness by using the power that already belongs to you. In other words, you don't have to emulate Sisyphus. There are other ways to move that boulder.

In Part One, I introduce you to your birthright: receptive power. I discuss what it is, how you can use it, and how cultural influences have interfered with your natural state.

In Part Two, I offer seven practical steps that you can easily integrate into your daily life. I give plenty of inspiring examples of women who have changed their lives for the better by using their receptive power. Each of the following steps includes exercises to help you put everything you have learned into practice:

- Step One: Pay Attention to Your Feelings and Trust Your Intuition
- Step Two: Know What You Want

- Step Three: Ask for Help If You Need It and Accept It When It's Offered

- Step Four: Be Grateful and Say Thank You

- Step Five: Create Full Reciprocity in Your Relationships

- Step Six: Don't Put Yourself Last or *You* Won't Last

- Step Seven: Be Respectful of Your Past, Have a Vision for Your Future, but Live in the Moment

You have the right to live a peaceful, meaningful, and fulfilling life. In the pages that follow, I give you the tools you need to reclaim your half of the universe. Now all you have to do is use them.

{ PART ONE }

You Were Born
to Receive

# The Language
of Receiving

Are you more comfortable giving than receiving? For many women, the answer is "yes." While you may have never thought about receiving as healthy and positive, the consequences of *not* receiving include the following:

- Emotionally, you feel unappreciated.
- Physically, you feel exhausted.
- Mentally, you feel resentful.
- Spiritually, you feel depleted.

It's like you have a gate that swings only one way, and all that you give doesn't bring anything back to you because the gate doesn't open toward you, only away from you.

Even though every giver has a receiver—there is a

recipient for every act of giving—we are taught to over-value one and devalue the other. It is not an accident that most people are unable to define the word "receive." The word itself is included in many lists of the top misspelled words. That's how little we use it and how unfamiliar we are, both men and women, with half of every exchange. Yet, receiving is not only natural, it is the partner of activity and it permeates every area of our lives.

# An Introduction to the Receptive World

## Definitions

Receive: to accept willingly

Receptive: ready or willing to receive

Receptivity: a willingness or readiness to receive

Reciprocity: a mode of exchange in which transactions take place between individuals who are symmetrically placed, i.e., they are exchanging as equals, neither being in a dominant position

## Receptive States

| | | |
|---|---|---|
| Meditating | Noticing | Appreciating |
| Listening | Smelling | Being |
| Tasting | Welcoming | Contemplating |
| Accepting | Yielding | Watching |
| Allowing | Including | Letting be |
| Opening | Embracing | Attracting |
| Relaxing | Feeling | Revealing |
| Letting go | Hearing | Acknowledging |

# Receptivities

*Receptivities* are the actions of a receptive state. Here are examples:

| A Receptive State | A Receptivity |
|---|---|
| Relaxing | Soaking in a hot bath |
| Appreciating | Sitting in your backyard admiring your garden |
| Tasting | Enjoying the flavor of your morning coffee |
| Noticing | People watching |

## When You Are in a Receptive State:

- You are calm, relaxed, and engaged.
- You conserve your energy and suspend activity.
- You listen.
- You remain open.
- You are patient.

## When You Balance Receptivity with Activity, Others See a Woman Who Is:

- Gracious
- Dignified
- Effective
- Attractive

# Forms of Reciprocity

*Relationship reciprocity* occurs when both people give and receive by:

- Helping each other
- Talking and listening
- Taking responsibility for the growth of the relationship
- Respecting each other

*Cultural reciprocity* describes a system that:

- Embraces the fluid blend of activity and receptivity that is reflected in all of nature
- Advocates for a movement toward balance and equality rather than force and domination
- Values receiving as much as giving
- Recognizes that the circle of life is completed and made whole when energy moves outward through activity and is returned via receptivity

*Social reciprocity* occurs when people give to and receive from a society. An example is when you give blood or volunteer for a charity. If you need blood or assistance, you receive the help you need. Since reciprocity is a term that denotes an exchange among equals, when a society discriminates against a group, the people from that group do not receive the benefits of the society to which they contribute.

*Environmental reciprocity* describes an ecosystem where collective survival is enhanced through interdependent relationships, many marked by cooperation and mutual exchange. Here are examples:

- Plants attract pollinators to drink the nectar that ensures their own continued existence.
- Plants and trees release the oxygen that we inhale, while they benefit from the carbon dioxide that we exhale.

- The delicate balance between predators and prey in the animal world improves the chances for mutual survival.

*Social environmental reciprocity* describes a relational approach to bringing Earth into environmental balance by putting back what you take out. This can be achieved by assessing your carbon footprint, figuring out your carbon dioxide contribution, and taking steps to offset it. Here are examples:

- Planting a tree
- Driving an electric car
- Choosing vegetarian or vegan diets or joining the Meatless Mondays movement
- Using energy-saving lightbulbs
- Investing in solar energy
- Buying green products

*Governmental reciprocity* occurs when the branches of a government both give and receive, working together for the benefit of the citizens. Additionally, citizens participate by both giving and receiving in their relationships with their representatives.

*Intergovernmental reciprocity* refers to the commercial and other dealings between two governments, by which corresponding advantages are granted by each country to the citizens of the other.

*Biological reciprocity* describes what occurs inside of your body. As an example: The cells in your body have receptors on their surface, which receive messages from molecules that attach to them. The communication that is received by the receptor tells the cell what to do. Receptors are very specialized and only certain molecules will "fit." The relationship between the receptor and the molecule that binds to it is like a lock-and-key system. They must be a perfect match for each other.

*Universal reciprocity* describes a holistic way of looking at life. You may have heard of the words yin (receptive) and yang (active), and you have probably seen the yin-yang symbol. It looks like this:

This philosophy presents a view of complementary, interconnected forces that are always in motion.

# { What Are Receptivities? }

**O**ur culture has little understanding of receptive states. Because of that, we don't have a nuanced vocabulary and certainly not one that has much appreciation or respect for what receptivity has to offer. People pride themselves on being busy and are suspicious of those who have too much time on their hands. We even have a saying: "Idle hands are the devil's playground."

But doesn't it make sense that if you give and give and give and don't receive from others, you end up depleted? Like anything in life, you need to fill back up what you have given out. You fill the car with gas when the gauge is on empty. If you don't, the car won't run. If you don't plug your computer, phones, and other electronic devices and appliances into a power source, they won't run either.

When you are in a receptive state, you may feel

like you are not really doing anything, or that you are not furthering your goals. But receptivity is a very dynamic state. When you are engaged in receptivities, you are in a fertile, creative territory.

Experts, books, and articles do a great job of explaining how you can reduce stress. They caution you not to add too much to your schedule. They describe the results that occur from doing too much and ask you to subtract some of your activities. They tell you what you can remove from your life. But what is in that space and time after the removal? Relaxation? How do you do it? What does that mean? Do you buy a hammock and crawl into it? Do you google "meditation" and locate a cave where you can escape the pressures of daily life? I believe a lot of us would relax if we only knew how.

When you enter a receptive state, you have not removed or reduced anything. You have added something. You are familiar with the word "activity" as being something that you do. In this book, I am asking you to divide this word into two categories to help you distinguish between the activities of an active state and the activities of a receptive state. To do that, I am going to invent a word or, more specifically, use a familiar word—"receptivity"—in a more concrete context. That way, you will be able to easily assess which of your activities are giving you energy and which ones are spending your energy. Here are examples:

- Hearing is a receptive state. Listening to music is a receptivity.

- Observing is a receptive state. Watching birds is a receptivity.

- Touching is a receptive state. Holding hands is a receptivity.

Let's look at this idea another way:

Activities = energy output

Receptivities = energy input

Activities speed you up and burn up your energy.

Receptivities slow you down and give you energy.

Activities are something you do when you expend energy.

Receptivities are something you do when you receive energy.

An easy way to distinguish whether you are engaging in an activity or a receptivity is to assess your energy output and input. If you invest in too much of one of them, you will throw yourself and your life out of balance. You will experience this in the following ways:

- If you do too many activities, you end up feeling burned out, worn down, and exhausted.

- If you do too many receptivities, you end up feeling lethargic, unmotivated, and uninterested in anything.

Receptivities not only balance activities, they complement them as well. For example, talking (an active state) has a partner, listening (a receptive state). If you practice listening then, when you are in a conversation, you will be better able to hear the other person. Listening receptivities include listening to birds sing, to the hum of a refrigerator, or to music, just to name a few.

## You Are Wired to Relax

Relaxation is not a pause between activities. It is its own thing. It's not idle time, not a waste of time, not a symptom of laziness, not something you do when you are sick, on a day when you don't have to work, or when you have run out of things to do.

The system that is in charge when your body is at rest is called the "parasympathetic nervous system" (PNS), also known as the "rest and digest" system. Its complement is the "sympathetic nervous system" (SNS), which stimulates the fight-or-flight response.

Think of the SNS as the accelerator and the PNS as the brake. Both are a part of the "autonomic nervous system," a system that regulates internal organs and glands. It makes common sense that they need to balance each other for overall health. Do you know people who have their foot on the accelerator 24/7, or couch potatoes who move only when they want to raid the fridge? It's easy to see the consequences of these extremes.

## Get to Know Your System

What fills you up or runs you down? Is your nervous system rock-solid or super-sensitive? Do you have loads of stamina? Do you feel energized when you are with people? Or do you have a delicate nervous system and feel easily drained if an environment is too stimulating or you have a lot of social interactions?

Depending on your system, you may need more or fewer receptivities to replenish your energy reserves. Some people need many receptivities every day to balance out their activities. Others do quite well with many activities and only a few receptivities. What is important is that you get the right ratio of activity to receptivity for your system. You may need to experiment to know what works for you. The following are examples of activities and receptivities:

### ACTIVITIES

- Driving
- Walking the dog
- Preparing food and cooking

- Washing dishes or loading the dishwasher
- Working
- Doing housework
- Washing, drying, and folding clothes
- Helping children with homework
- Making appointments
- Grocery shopping
- Mowing the lawn
- Making phone calls and texting
- Checking your email and social media
- Posting, blogging, and tweeting
- Paying bills
- Taking the trash out

## RECEPTIVITIES

- Reading a book, newspaper, magazine, or online content
- Sleeping
- Resting
- Soaking in a bathtub
- Meditating
- Doing yoga, tai chi, or qigong
- Listening to music
- Spending time in nature

- Petting your cat or dog
- Watching birds
- Writing in a gratitude journal
- Puttering
- Doodling
- Looking at the ocean, a river, a lake, or a pond
- Admiring flowers

Once you figure out how many activities and receptivities you need each day, make a list. If you find yourself filling up on too many activities, replace some of them with receptivities. You can delegate some of the activities, or save them for another day.

I hope you are beginning to understand that receptivity isn't a values-based decision, as in "I'll receive this good thing but not that bad one." Receiving is not about cherry-picking what you want to receive. Nor does receiving have anything to do with your feelings about yourself or your beliefs about the world. Receiving is a natural part of life. It's in your biology, in the environment, in everything.

# The ABCs of Receiving

Receiving is a skill that can be learned, developed, and strengthened. Readers of my first book will recognize the following three exercises that I covered extensively in *The Power of Receiving*. With consistent daily practice, you will easily be able to recognize and receive what people and the world have to offer you. Integrate them into your daily life and there will be little that is not yours for the asking.

ACCEPT ALL COMPLIMENTS

BE SPIRITUALLY NAKED

COUNT YOUR BLESSINGS

## Accept All Compliments

A huge connection exists between what you are willing to receive and what you actually get. Show the world that you are ready to receive.

- Receive what is given to you, including compliments, smiles, and gifts.
- Accept them graciously and with gratitude.
- Once you receive the "little" things, you will easily graduate to the "bigger" ones.

## Be Spiritually Naked

Share who you are with others and invite them to get to know you. If you embrace your wholeness, others will, too.

- Be self-revealing. Don't showcase only the healed or "together" parts of your personality.
- Look for opportunities to let people know what is going on with you.
- Be authentic, be transparent, be real.

## Count Your Blessings

Gratitude is a state of mind and a way of seeing life. Strengthen your receptive powers by focusing on what you are grateful for.

- Look for reasons to be grateful.
- Be genuinely appreciative.
- Say "thank you."

# The Top Ten Features of Skilled Receivers

1. A receiver knows how to accept a compliment graciously and is genuinely pleased to receive it.

2. A receiver regularly expresses gratitude.

3. A receiver's attention is on the present rather than dwelling on the past or fretting about the future.

4. A receiver is a good listener.

5. A receiver is observant.

6. A receiver defines a "good person" as a whole person rather than as someone who places other people's needs above her own.

7. A receiver does not enable people.

8. A receiver knows when to cease activity.

9. A receiver utilizes data in her environment to help her make decisions.

10. A receiver doesn't complain.

# What Is Receptive Power?

**Active power:** Creating change through activity or force

**Receptive power:** Creating change by withdrawing support or by calling attention to a problem or solution

We women don't like conflict. We're not the sort to draw a line in the sand, challenging someone to cross it. We don't like to run rough-shod over people. Not our style. In fact, when conflict arises, many of us run in the other direction with sweaty palms.

Being conflict-averse, how can we advocate for what we want when confronted with disagreeable people and those who refuse to listen to us, consider our needs, or respect what we want?

Have you ever argued with someone and noticed

that the calmer you remained, the louder, more domineering, and strident the other person became? There you are—quiet, immovable, relaxed. You are open, you are listening, and you are sure of yourself. That's receptive power. It has worn down people and it has worn down nations.

### You use receptive power when you:

- Remain calm when another person is riled up
- Listen to what someone has to say, even if you disagree
- Insist that others speak respectfully to you, and are willing to walk away if they don't
- Refuse to do something that goes against your values, morals, or beliefs
- Advocate for your own needs
- Withhold something that the other person wants until they meet you halfway
- Stand up for yourself
- Don't give up

### We use receptive power as a social tool when we:

- Boycott
- Commit acts of civil disobedience
- Engage in peaceful resistance

- Go on a hunger strike
- Include others by inviting them to join us to help find a solution

Personal example: A woman uses receptive power when she refuses to clean up after family members who won't do their fair share of housework.

Social example: Rosa Parks, a Civil Rights heroine, committed an act of civil disobedience when she refused to give up her seat on the bus to a white passenger.

## Staying Power

Many women give up too easily when asking for what they want. Just the other day, a friend told me (and she is a doctor with plenty of authority in the work arena) that when she asked her unemployed husband to grocery shop, he said no. My friend shrugged her shoulders. "What can I do? I can't make him do it," she told me. It's no accident that my friend is a busy multitasker.

What do you do when you are stumped by someone's refusal to meet you halfway? Do you argue? Do you negotiate? Do you insist? Or do you just give up?

When most, if not all, of your energy is invested in doing and giving with little or no expectation of reciprocity, do you see how easily you and your relationships can be thrown out of balance?

In contrast, when you use receptive power, you are calm, are patient, and possess a steady determination. You tap into receptive power when you step back and observe your environment and the people in it. You utilize receptive power when you tune in to your feelings and allow them to contribute to your decisions.

Those who use receptive power, socially or personally, do not give up. Their stamina, strength, and willingness to stay the course, even in the face of hardship, wins them a better life and one in which everybody benefits—women and men.

Because of fear of conflict, many of your needs, desires, and dreams are never fulfilled simply because you do not stand your ground and remain committed to what you know in your heart and soul is right for you.

Receptive power is the feminine half of creation. When you use your receptive power at the right time, in the right place, with the right people, you create balance in your relationships and in your life.

# The CULTure of
# Self-Esteem

N ancy, the head of an organization that sponsors workshops, told me that she has asked a roomful of women on more than one occasion to raise their hands if they were comfortable accepting a compliment. "No one raises their hands," she told me. "Not one woman!"

I was not surprised to hear this. Ask a woman to accept a compliment, and you can easily end up in a discussion about her feelings of unworthiness or hear from her about the lack of merit of the compliment she has been given. "I have low self-esteem," women say over and over. It's like everybody has been drinking the same Kool-Aid.

The reality is that feelings are not static. They shift and change throughout an hour, a day, a week, a year, and a lifetime. I don't feel confident about myself 100 percent of the time. Neither do I feel insecure or anxious 100 percent of the time.

If I decided that my self-worth had to be in tip-top shape in the exact moment that I received a compliment or other gift, I would be in danger of having to refuse much of the good that comes my way! Nobody feels super-über great about themselves 100 percent of the time. Nobody. Not men. Not women.

Doesn't it seem strange, if you think about it, that a person's response to a compliment is that she doesn't feel worthy of accepting it? There are so many terrible, heart-wrenching situations and events that occur in the world every day. You would think we would be relieved that there are people thoughtful enough to extend the kindness of a compliment. You'd think that we would be grateful.

Doesn't it also seem strange that this habitual refusal is almost always from women? Can you imagine eavesdropping on a group of men, finding them engaged in a discussion about their battle with self-esteem, their struggle to feel confident, or their hurt feelings about who was saying what about them?

Men do not feel that they have to constantly shore up their self-esteem to be effective in the world or to achieve the things they want. In fact, most men do not think about the state of their self-esteem. Ever.

Low self-esteem, if we are to believe the messages we constantly hear, is due to our gender. Have I missed something? Is there an "I'm unworthy" gene?

Where did this idea come from, that we should strive for this Holy Grail of self-esteem? And why do we think a lack of self-esteem is an internal defect to be examined and ignore the external factors—those institutions and people who deride and bully us? Why do we talk about it at all?

## Getting a Girl to Feel Bad about Herself Is Like Shooting Fish in a Barrel

Children are no match for an advertising industry that targets them, purposefully whittling down their confidence and self-esteem just so that they can sell products to make money.

But why are women vulnerable to this manipulation? And worse, why are we allowing advertisers to have access to our daughters even as we experience the erosion of our own self-esteem? Too many of us are enabling predatory businesses to make money at the emotional expense and well-being of our children. The fact that they do this is reprehensible. The fact that we allow it is mystifying.

No wonder girls and women feel it is *natural* to have low self-esteem. We are constantly told that we struggle with self-esteem and that there are products and tips that will help us. It's become a mantra that women repeat over and over: *I have low self-worth. I have low self-worth.*

Although these external cultural forces have their hooks in us and continually try to hypnotize us into believing there is something wrong with us, you must not allow this to affect how you feel about yourself. If you believe these abusers, you will not think there is something wrong with *them*, you will think something is wrong with *you*. But this is a child's way to think, and women are not children—right?

## This Is Why You Think You Have Low Self-Esteem

Children blame themselves when adults abuse them. In their young, immature minds they believe, "It's my fault. There's something wrong with me. If I were different, my parents would love me." When we grow up, we realize that we didn't do something wrong, the adults did something harmful.

This is what we, as grown women, are doing. We don't look at the external forces of manipulation and abuse; instead, we blame ourselves. "If I were prettier, smarter, thinner, or more perfect, people would treat me better, love me, and accept me." This is a mass cultural illusion. And our response to it is childlike, it's immature.

I believe that our tepid collective response to this assault on our well-being is a result of the fact that having economic and legal rights is still relatively new for us. Maturity is gained by experience and having responsibilities, by making our own decisions. I believe our emotions have not caught up to modern times, to the twenty-first century.

While women won the right to vote in 1920, and subsequent laws have helped women inch toward equality, it wasn't until the 1970s that a series of laws was passed that gave women a large number of important legal and economic rights, including the right to get a bank loan, a mortgage, or a credit card under their own name. Until we had those rights, we weren't really grown-ups. Men were, for better or worse, our protectors, our mediators, our guardians of the world. No wonder our maturity has lagged. Until relatively recently, we've had no more rights than children.

I want to be clear that I am not advocating that we should never look into our inner workings and process events that have been difficult. Many of us are very willing to examine our psyches and are, by far, the majority of consumers of therapeutic services. But correctly identifying the source of a problem is a major part of healing and of emotional development.

## Receiving Is Mechanistic

I want to make one last point about self-esteem (for the time being, at least). In over two decades of researching the topic of receiving, I have discovered that the act of receiving has nothing to do with how you feel about yourself. Let me explain.

To receive is to accept willingly. When someone pays you a compliment, your own opinion about yourself in that moment does not matter. Giving and receiving together is a circle of energy, of activity and receptivity. It is a natural exchange that is reflected in all of nature, in our biology, and in our psychology. You can witness this in the giving and receiving of a flower and its pollinators, in the molecules that lock on to receptors, and in the talking and listening that occurs in a conversation. In each of these examples, one wonders: Who is the giver and who is the receiver?

A flower does not need to feel good about itself to attract a butterfly. A cell does not have a receptor because it is confident. A listener can be receptive no matter what she is feeling in that moment. Receiving is not dependent upon your opinion of yourself.

When you push away a compliment instead of receiving it, you are doing something that is unnatural. The ripple effects of that refusal have consequences in all areas of your life.

Don't allow your sense of self to be dictated by those who do not have your best interests in mind, who don't have your back. Make a commitment today to never, ever again say out loud or to yourself, "I feel unworthy. I have low self-esteem." Then watch the miracles in your life unfold.

{ **PART TWO** }

Seven Steps to
Reclaim Your Half
of the Universe

# Pay Attention to
# Your Feelings and Trust
# Your Intuition

A friend recently told me that when the counselor at a rehab center asked how she felt about her son's addiction, she didn't know how to answer because she didn't know how she felt. "How can I not know how I feel about my son's addiction?" she asked me.

How *did* feelings, one of women's greatest natural gifts, become so inaccessible? We are born with a rich, informative, exciting world at our beck and call—except we don't call, and even worse, when a feeling taps us on the shoulder or whispers to our heart, we ignore it.

How many times have you known something

didn't feel right but never paused to pay attention—
dismissing a feeling that has mercifully arrived to help you
before you listened to what it wants to tell you? No wonder
our feelings are hard to reach. Who would want to hang
around someone who kept ignoring you?

In the late seventies, I almost got myself killed in New
York City because I dismissed a feeling. The city was so
dangerous back then that almost everyone had a hair-
raising story to tell. One day as I entered my apartment
building, two men asked me to hold the door for them and
I did even though something didn't feel right. I walked up
the stairs ahead of the eerily quiet men. When I reached the
first landing, one of them held a gun to my head while they
robbed me. I learned later at the police station that a lot of
women had been followed into their apartment buildings
and robbed by the same men.

When I told my friends about what had happened to me,
they weren't surprised since rapes, robberies, muggings,
and even crimes as brazen as necklaces being grabbed from
necks in broad daylight, happened so frequently. I wish I
had known then that we didn't have to be such easy marks.
I wish we had made listening to our feelings and trusting
our intuition a priority.

I am not surprised that we have such a hard time access-
ing our feelings, since many of us have been raised to believe that our feelings aren't important. Have you ever been

told to stop being so emotional? Perhaps you've given up telling people how you feel because they don't listen to you. Maybe you are used to hearing, "You don't feel that way," or "Don't let it upset you." Or, perhaps people tell you how you *should* feel, instead of accepting how you actually feel. Over time, it's easy to become unwitting conspirators in rejecting our feelings.

If I had a dollar for every time I've ignored a feeling throughout my life, I would be a wealthy woman! These days I am in awe of their power and their all-around helpfulness. And because of that, I've made a vow to treat these valuable messengers with the respect they deserve. It is my hope that, after you finish this chapter, you will make the same vow.

In the pages that follow, I show you how and why welcoming your feelings helps you to know what you want, to be a good judge of character, to cultivate reciprocity in your relationships, and to create good health. At the end of this chapter, I have exercises that help you identify your feelings, listen to them, and consider them when you make decisions.

## A Vocabulary of Feelings

How many words do you have for what you feel? As a guardian of the feeling world, you need to know them. Even if others diminish, demean, or dismiss your feelings, *you* must not. Not knowing how you feel puts you at an extreme disadvantage. When you get to know your feelings just as you would a person, you make smart decisions that help you.

## List of Feelings

| | |
|---|---|
| Happy | Delighted |
| Sad | Compassionate |
| Hopeful | Unsympathetic |
| Discouraged | Confident |
| Loving | Insecure |
| Uncaring | Content |
| Appreciative | Depressed |
| Envious | Greedy |
| Angry | Generous |
| Joyful | Impatient |
| Anxious | Patient |
| Calm | Irritable |
| Afraid | Even-tempered |
| Courageous | Inspired |
| Disgusted | Bored |

You and everybody else have experienced every feeling on this list. It's part of being human. But if you are like a lot of people, you have been taught that some of these feelings are unacceptable. Here are some of the reasons why you may ignore some of your feelings while treating others as golden children:

- You don't want to "rock the boat."

- You don't want to make others unhappy.

- You don't want to disappoint someone.

- You fear your feelings will overwhelm you.

- You think if you pay attention to them, you will have to do something you don't want to do.

- You believe if you focus on a difficult feeling, it will strengthen and grow.

- You worry that expressing your feelings will lead to conflict.

- You simply don't make a habit of paying attention to your feelings.

The next section examines those feelings that, although they may be the easiest to push away, are the ones that most need your attention, caring, and companionship. They are the ones that will liberate you.

# Receive Everything—
# Decide Later

If you ignore a feeling, it doesn't disappear, just as people you dislike don't vanish into thin air because you don't pay any attention to them. Yet, you may think—or hope—that if you ignore certain feelings, they will go away.

Recently, I spoke with a client whose dog had died. She told me she kept as busy as possible so that she could keep the grief away. But ignoring her feelings didn't make them leave or even lessen them. Instead, unacknowledged grief stayed close by, waiting for an opportunity to be with her. I felt sympathy for my client, but I also felt sorry for the feelings she wouldn't let in.

All feelings are valuable messengers. They tell you whether something feels good or bad. They help you make decisions about what you want to do, with whom you want to spend time, and where you want to go.

Are you worried that if you acknowledge a feeling it will move into your house, raid the fridge, and unfurl its sleeping bag? Are you concerned that you will never get rid of it? In reality, getting to know a feeling and listening to what it has to say will help it move along. Appreciating it helps it move faster. It has messages for more people than just you. That's what is so wonderful about our shared humanity.

Every feeling you have is felt by everybody else. Everybody. That feeling doesn't want to get trapped, hanging around like a stalker trying to avoid a restraining order. It just wants to deliver its message. Let it. It's there to help you.

If you receive and welcome your feelings, they won't feel like they have to pursue, nag, or clobber you to get your attention.

- You don't have to be their best friend.
- You don't have to love them.
- You don't have to know what to do with them.
- You don't have to explain them.
- You don't have to justify them.
- You don't have to have an opinion about them.

Just receive them. You can decide later what to do with what you have received.

## Drama Queens, Ice Queens, and In-Betweens

If you buy a lottery ticket and don't win, do you break down, cry, and scream about the unfairness of it all? Hopefully not! But I'll bet you've met more than a few Drama

Queens who pitch a fit when people don't do what they want them to do or something doesn't go the way they want it to go. Television shows love to showcase their bad behavior. It seems they're everywhere these days.

At the opposite end of the continuum are the emotionally distant Ice Queens, who reveal little to nothing about what they think or feel, or even what they plan to do. Ice Queens are high-achieving perfectionists who are top performers in their careers and supermoms at home. Although they are not as ubiquitous as Drama Queens, television loves to feature a frosty villainess, and you've probably met a few of these haughty queens.

You might think that Drama Queens are way too in touch with their feelings, while Ice Queens could benefit from a good spring thaw. But the truth is, neither one sits with a feeling long enough to get to know it. Instead, they freak out or shut down. In addition to running away from their feelings, they also share the following:

- Both have difficulty establishing healthy boundaries.
- Both have poor judgment when assessing people or situations.
- Both have trouble establishing reciprocity in their relationships.
- Both frequently criticize others—Drama Queens complain loudly and Ice Queens judge silently.

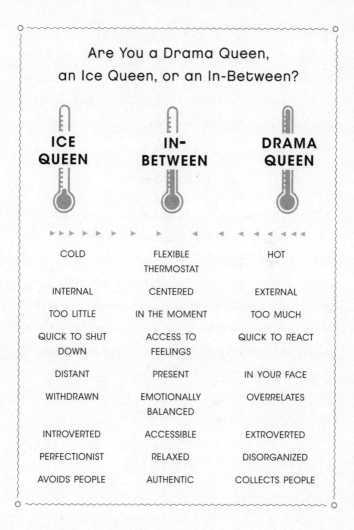

Are You a Drama Queen,
an Ice Queen, or an In-Between?

| ICE QUEEN | IN-BETWEEN | DRAMA QUEEN |
|---|---|---|
| COLD | FLEXIBLE THERMOSTAT | HOT |
| INTERNAL | CENTERED | EXTERNAL |
| TOO LITTLE | IN THE MOMENT | TOO MUCH |
| QUICK TO SHUT DOWN | ACCESS TO FEELINGS | QUICK TO REACT |
| DISTANT | PRESENT | IN YOUR FACE |
| WITHDRAWN | EMOTIONALLY BALANCED | OVERRELATES |
| INTROVERTED | ACCESSIBLE | EXTROVERTED |
| PERFECTIONIST | RELAXED | DISORGANIZED |
| AVOIDS PEOPLE | AUTHENTIC | COLLECTS PEOPLE |

You may not identify as a Drama Queen or an Ice Queen, but how many times have you overreacted or mentally checked out so quickly that it wasn't until later that you realized your behavior didn't fit the situation? Or, perhaps in retrospect, you recognized that you didn't see or hear something that would have helped you to respond more appropriately. It's so easy to make a mess of things by treating people in a way that has nothing to do with them.

## Drama Queens

A Drama Queen wants to be the center of attention and is a collector of people—her audience. She speaks in a loud voice, is frequently hyper, dominates conversations, and is in charge of the itinerary. She ties her well-being to people who go along with what she wants and opts out of situations she cannot control. She falls apart when she is ignored or when things don't go the way she wants them to go. It's tempting to give in to a Drama Queen. She throws a tantrum if she doesn't get her way, she complains, and she doesn't let up until she gets what she wants. If you know a Drama Queen, you may have concluded that it's just not worth it to disagree with her.

## Ice Queens

Meeting an Ice Queen is like encountering a sheet of ice. You can't get any traction with her. She has few facial expressions and her stoic mask betrays nothing about what is going on inside of her. She frequently comes across as haughty and arrogant and lets you know that she doesn't care about what you think of her. She is proud of being self-sufficient and is often found in professions where she is in charge. An Ice Queen has a hard time trusting people and, because of that, has few friends.

## In-Betweens

Most of us are In-Betweens——overreacting sometimes and emotionally shutting down at other times. An In-Between has greater flexibility overall and is able to catch herself when she realizes that she has responded inappropriately. If you are self-aware enough to know, even in hindsight, when you have overreacted or shut down to a person or situation, you are an In-Between. Drama Queens and Ice Queens are full of excuses for their behavior and blame others for their reactions. In-Betweens avail themselves of the support of others and of information that can help them to be happy human beings.

## A Flexible Thermostat

The closer you are to the center of the thermostat (an In-Between), the more likely you are to respond in the moment to what is happening in that moment. If something doesn't feel right, you pay attention. If you get a good feeling, you pay attention to that, too. The more flexible your thermostat, the more open and receptive you are to people, situations, and events. You don't have to wonder how you feel, you *know* how you feel.

A flexible thermostat gives you access to your feelings, and when you are in this open receptive state:

- You consciously respond rather than react to what is in front of you.
- You pay attention if something does or doesn't feel right.
- You trust that a feeling has valuable information.
- You trust your feelings in the moment.
- You are in the moment when the moment occurs.

I told a friend that I was writing a chapter about how important it is for women to pay attention to and act on their feelings. She told me the following story:

When she was in her twenties, she had accepted a job. This job was not in her chosen profession (film and theater). A few days after she started working, she received an invitation for a job in the film industry, which was everything she had worked toward and longed for. But because she felt that she could not go back on her word, she turned down the exciting opportunity and continued to work in the job that meant nothing to her, in which she could have been easily replaced.

She told me that turning down that job was one of her greatest regrets. She felt that her destiny had come calling, knocking on her door, and that she had not opened it. She went on to create a fulfilling life, but she always wondered what would have happened if she had made her feelings important.

Here is an example of a woman who paid attention to her feelings:

When Rosa Parks refused to give up her bus seat so that a white person could sit down, she sparked the Montgomery Bus Boycott and became one of the civil rights movement's most famous heroines.

In a 1992 interview with National Public Radio's Lynn Neary, Parks recalled, "I did not want to be mistreated, I did not want to be deprived of a seat that I had paid for. It was just time . . . there was opportunity for me to take a stand to express the way I felt about being treated in that manner. I had not planned to get arrested. I had plenty to do without having to end up in jail. But when I had to face that decision, I didn't hesitate to do so, because I felt that we had endured that too long. The more we gave in, the more we complied with that kind of treatment, the more oppressive it became."

Is there something that you endure? Do you keep your

mouth closed when someone disrespects you? Do you push down your feelings because speaking up would risk conflict, cause discomfort, or disappoint someone?

Here's another example of a woman who honored her feelings:

Leslie slowed down a relationship she felt she had jumped into too quickly. Her partner wasn't happy about it. "I feel like you pulled the rug out from under me," he said.

"I feel bad that he's sad, but I'm finally not taking responsibility for someone else's emotions like I usually have done," Leslie told me. "In the past, I tended to give, give, give too much of me, but at the expense of me. Some of that giving was the natural me, yet some of that giving may have been not so healthy—giving too much slack to inappropriate behavior, or giving one too many chances to start over."

If you make your feelings important enough to pay attention to, other people can't help but pay attention also. The next time you catch yourself overreacting or shutting down, pause, take a deep breath, adjust your thermostat, and move into a receptive state.

## The Role of Intuition

When you drill down into a feeling, logic helps you connect a situation or person to how you feel. Intuition is different. It's a feeling that you can't explain. Intuition is when you get a hunch, a vibe, or a premonition that doesn't make logical sense. Intuition is often present in those decisions that turn your life in a positive direction such as a hunch to take a certain job, or move to a new area, or contact a particular person.

Intuition is also at work when the hairs on the back of your neck stand up when you are in the presence of someone who otherwise seems perfectly nice. It's at work when you walk into a room and feel like you need to get out. But if anybody asked you why, you would be hard-pressed to explain your reason.

## Have You Spent Time with a Future "Person of Interest"?

Many of us are very good at tending to people's needs and helping them to feel comfortable. This gift can put us in a difficult position if our intuition tells us that someone is bad news. A lot of us don't want to hurt anyone's feelings. Have you ever overridden your natural instinct for survival by doing any of the following?

- Have you stepped into an elevator with a man you didn't know because you didn't want to hurt his feelings or make him feel uncomfortable?

- Have you ever stayed in a relationship even though you feared your partner may hurt or even kill you?

- Have you ever remained in a relationship with someone who emotionally, verbally, or physically abused you?

- Have you ever gotten into a car with someone who made you nervous?

Gavin De Becker, a leading expert on violent behavior, listed thirty pre-indicators of violence and murder in his book *The Gift of Fear*. Here's number one: The woman has an intuitive feeling that she is at risk.

Your intuition is one of your most valuable gifts. If you practice paying attention to those hunches, vibes, and sixth-sense feelings, you will become skilled at being able to read people and situations accurately. That, in turn, will help you make positive changes in your life.

## A Complaint Fast

When I left the gym the other day, I passed by a group of girls who looked to be around ten years old. One of them was complaining loudly about a buckle on her backpack. She didn't like it. The others nodded in sympathy. I walked a little farther and heard two women complaining about a coworker who wasn't doing her share of the workload.

We live in a society where complaining is a way of life

and a way to bond. But recounting the unfairnesses, the slights, and the difficulties that you endure day in and day out has insidious consequences. Complaints are not only toxic. This personal polluting factory also prevents you from experiencing your feelings. And feeling your feelings is what will lead you to a new life.

Complaining is different from talking about your feelings. Complaining is telling a story about your suffering. And as you have probably discovered, that story doesn't ever seem to end! Additionally, it chases people away. Have you ever been trapped listening to a monologue of misery? It's not fun.

Feelings are universal; everyone can relate to them. When you talk or write about your feelings, you discover solutions that help you find your way to a happier situation.

I have a motto: *No suffering allowed! No suffering aloud!* The next time you have an impulse to complain, stop! Within a week, your feelings and intuition will point you in a direction and lead you to people who will help you create a life in which you feel happy and fulfilled.

Are you ready to reclaim your half of the universe? The following exercises will get you started.

{ EXERCISES }

## 1. SPEND TIME WITH YOUR FEELINGS

Write down your feelings about the following people and places. You probably have more than one feeling, and you may have conflicting feelings. That's okay. Life would be simple if we had only one feeling per person. We don't live in that world. So write down as many feelings that apply.

These are my feelings about my job:

_____

_____

These are my feelings about my relationship:

_____

_____

These are my feelings about my mom:

_____

_____

These are my feelings about my child:

_____

_____

These are my feelings about my house:

_____

_____

These are my feelings about my health:

_____

_____

These are my feelings about what is going on in the world:

_____

_____

These are my feelings about (fill in your own):

_____

_____

## 2. BUILD AND STRENGTHEN YOUR FEELING RECEPTORS

Choose one feeling and spend the day with it. Make a point to notice every time you see that feeling expressed, whether in you or in someone else. Don't form an opinion about it. Don't judge it. Just notice it. This exercise is designed to help you recognize feelings as they occur in you or in someone else. Here is an example:

*Kindness:* Every time you see someone say or do something that is kind, note it, remember it, write it down in a journal or notebook. (I have created a *Power of Receiving Journal.* You can find information about it at www.AmandaOwen.com.) What are the circumstances and who is the person expressing kindness? Who is the recipient? Where did this take place?

Do this same exercise with feelings that are uncomfortable. For example, choose the feeling "anger" and note it every time you witness it in you or in someone else throughout a day.

What this exercise does is strengthen your capacity to recognize feelings as they occur in you and in others in the moment that they occur. You will then become able to respond in a way that helps you.

## 3. RECEIVE EVERYTHING—DECIDE LATER

Too often, we chase away a feeling because we think we will have to do something about it. But we don't. Use the statement *Receive everything—decide later* as a reminder to pause, wait, and pay attention to what you are feeling. You can do this anywhere—in your car while you are driving to work, when you are walking your dog, or when you are put on hold during a phone conversation. Don't worry about what you will do with what you feel or even about your thoughts about your feelings. Just receive them. You can de-cide later what you want to do with them.

## 4. MAINTAIN A FLEXIBLE THERMOSTAT

When you want to freak out or shut down, check in with your feelings instead. You don't need to say any-thing or ignore anything. Just be present, engaged, and genuine. Your feelings and your intuition need your attention, and now is the time to pay attention to them.

## 5. COMMIT TO A COMPLAINT FAST

Start with spending one day without complaining. If you have an impulse to complain, check in with your feelings instead. Sit with them a bit. Become familiar with what they are telling you. Enlist help from people you know. Some people ask their family to commit to the Complaint Fast. Others create a "complaint-free zone" at work.

## { INSPIRING QUOTES }

*My moods are continuously shifting like the weather.*

○ PEMA CHÖDRÖN ○

*Intuition is a spiritual faculty and does not explain,
but simply points the way.*

○ FLORENCE SCOVEL SHINN ○

*The deepest feeling always shows itself in silence.*

○ MARIANNE MOORE ○

*Don't let anyone tell you that you have to be
a certain way. Be unique. Be what you feel.*

○ MELISSA ETHERIDGE ○

*Feelings are your guide. Trust your feelings and
learn to express them, and do not blame anyone for
how you feel. Be yourself, observe yourself.*

○ BARBARA MARCINIAK ○

*You must train your intuition——you must trust*
*the small voice inside you which tells*
*you exactly what to say, what to decide.*

∘ INGRID BERGMAN ∘

*Lesson one, follow your feelings. If it feels right,*
*move forward. If it doesn't feel right, don't do it.*

∘ OPRAH WINFREY ∘

## Know What You Want

A dog trainer on a TV show called *Dogs in the City* asked a woman, whose dog jumped on people the minute they entered her apartment, what she wanted her dog to do.

"I don't want him to jump on people," the woman said.

"What do you want him to do?" the dog trainer asked.

"I don't want him to jump on people anymore."

"Not what you *don't* want—what *do* you want?"

"Oh," she said. "I want him to sit about ten feet away, over by the couch."

"Got it!" he said. "Now we have something we can work with."

Do you know more about what you *don't* want than what you *do* want? Lots of people talk about what they don't want as their default. Days, weeks, months, and even years can pass by while thinking: *Get me out of this job! I don't want to be in this relationship! I don't want to live in this house!*

A friend of mine has complained for years about her "soul-destroying" job. She desperately wants to leave. But day after day and year after year, there she sits in her soul-destroying job.

Unfortunately, her situation is not unusual. Why do so many women remain in jobs, relationships, and other situations that are unfulfilling and even, as my friend put it, soul-destroying?

I believe this occurs because women don't have enough practice wanting. *Huh?* Some of you might say that we live in a greedy, grabby, entitled society, and the idea that people could use practice in wanting sounds—well, out of touch. But hear me out.

Do you pay more attention to other people's needs than to your own? Do you talk more about your children, grandchildren, or mate than about yourself? Have you even thought lately about what you want? Do you feel uncomfortable asking for what you want unless the following conditions are met?

- What you want doesn't make others uncomfortable, upset, or angry.

- What you want doesn't interfere with what people want for themselves.

- What you want doesn't interfere with what someone else wants for you.

- Others approve of what you want.

Wanting something for yourself is as natural as wanting something for someone else. But if you are not in the habit of paying attention to your desires, doesn't it make sense that you will not know what you want, let alone ask for or get what you want? Have you ever been asked what you want and been unable to answer the question?

## The Art of Wanting

In Step One, I spoke about the harmful consequences of complaining. When you constantly focus on what you don't like and don't want, you see the world through a grimy lens. That view will not lead you to a better life.

I am not asking you to be happy about circumstances in which you are unhappy. I am asking you to create a picture in your mind of a wonderful, beautiful image of you—happy and content. I am asking you to create something to aim for.

I'll tell you a story from my own life. Years ago, I smoked three packs of cigarettes every day. When I reached my late thirties, I didn't want to be a smoker anymore. I obsessed endlessly about this. *I don't want to smoke! I have to stop smok-ing! This is so unhealthy! I have to find a way to stop!*

I started smoking when I was fourteen years old because I wanted to be with the "cool" kids who gathered in a field behind the school each day. They smoked cigarettes and wore leather jackets—such an exciting world. Sign me up!

Two decades later, as I fretted about my smoking habit, I wondered what I would do if I didn't smoke. *What would my life look like? Who would I be?* I didn't know how to answer these questions. Not a clue.

I decided to create a detailed picture in my mind of how I thought I, as a healthy person, might look. I visualized my-self straddling a bicycle (I never rode bikes), holding a tennis racket (I never played tennis), with a smiling sun-kissed face (I didn't spend much time outside), wearing sneakers (I al-ways wore boots).

I tweaked this image over time, and after a while I began to like this new me. It took about a year, but I finally began my life as a nonsmoker on April 28, 1993.

Take the time to figure out what you want. Desire is a catalyst for change. Naming it gets you started.

## Want ~ Ask ~ Receive

Alice Paul knew what she wanted—an amendment to the U.S. Constitution giving women the right to vote. She asked for it over and over and over again. When one method didn't move the cause forward, Alice switched to another tactic. When one organization did not support her cause, she left and created another organization. She kept looking for receptive people, receptive organizations, receptive politicians, and a receptive president. And she found them. She utilized nonviolent protest, civil disobedience, hunger strikes, and picketing. She kept the pressure on Congress and on the president.

In 1918, President Wilson urged Congress to pass the legislation to amend the Constitution. In 1919, Congress submitted the amendment to the states for ratification. And finally, in 1920, the Nineteenth Amendment, which prohibits any United States citizen to be denied the right to vote based on sex, was ratified.

## What Do You Want?

### Do these examples sound familiar?

- I want you to clean your room.
- I want you to treat me better.
- I want a new job.
- I want you to help me.
- I want to sell my house.
- I want peace in the world.

- I want my cat to use the litter box.
- I want to grow my own vegetables.
- I want to get more sleep.

Every single day you have a list of wants, whether you want a particular food from the grocery store or you hit a snooze alarm because you want more sleep. Desire is a part of being human. You can't get away from it.

Yet many women are uncomfortable saying what they want for themselves. Do you make excuses for your unwillingness to ask for what you want? Are you reluctant to express a preference? Do you adopt a philosophical attitude as an excuse for not saying what you want? Here are some of the statements I have heard:

- I am fine. I don't really need anything.
- The Universe/God will provide.
- If I say what I want, it won't do any good since no one listens to me.

First, everybody has needs. Don't make a habit of denying them. Instead, take the time to become familiar with your desires and preferences. Once you know what they are, you will be able to speak about them.

Second, if you gave 100 percent of all decision making to God or the Universe, you would need to count on the

Universe/God to push the snooze alarm, shop for you, and talk to the cat about that litter box issue. Make sure you don't have a list of one—you—as the only person for whom it is unseemly or ungodly to want, ask, and receive.

Third, asking for anything invites the risk of rejection. Getting everything you ask for can't be your objective. No healthy relationship is about getting everything you want. If it was, you would never ask for anything unless you could predict the outcome. The point of asking is to become comfortable with not only stating your needs, but also with the fact that you *do* have needs.

Give yourself permission to explore your wants, needs, preferences, and desires. You don't have to make any decisions about them. You don't have to act on them. Just get to know them.

○ ○ ○

MANY WOMEN WHO do not know what they want are very familiar with other people's desires and are quite skilled at helping them get what they want.

- Are you helping your spouse get a college degree?
- Are you helping your child become a singing star?
- Are you helping your boss look good to his or her superiors?

- Are you helping your coworkers with their work?
- Are you helping a friend get her business off the ground?

I am not saying that there is anything wrong with helping people get what they want. We would all benefit if people thought a little less about themselves and a lot more about others. But, the truth is, whether it's because of our biology or social conditioning, many of us regularly think about other people's needs and desires. The problem is that, too often, we do it at the expense of our own. Then we wake up one day and realize that we don't have a clue about what we want.

Here is an example:

When Nadine saw that her boyfriend was struggling with his business, she was happy to pitch in and help. She had a business that offered the services he needed and she thought they would become closer if they worked together. She added these new tasks onto her already busy schedule. Just as in many of these kinds of situations, she soon discovered that the more she helped him, the more he took her for granted.

After several months, she found out that he was continuing to pay the woman who had previously done everything she was now doing. When she asked him about it, he said he knew she needed the money. *So do I,* Nadine thought.

Nadine realized she needed to get clear about what she wanted. What she knew for sure at this point was that she didn't want to work for free while he continued to pay someone for not working! After taking the time to figure out what she wanted, she approached him with a business proposition: She would continue to do the job she had been doing, if he paid her to do it. They worked out the details and she is now doing an excellent job helping him with his business.

Here is another example:

When Anne saw on Facebook that I was writing a chapter called "Know What You Want," she sent me an email. "I've recently come to appreciate what a big block I have had around wanting anything. It's not so easy to know what you want. I've had to learn to listen to myself, as I had gotten accustomed to going along with whatever anyone else wanted."

I can relate to what Anne is saying. It's easy to make a habit of not choosing. I used to do the same thing. If a boyfriend asked what restaurant I wanted to go to, I asked him where he wanted to go. If a friend asked me what time I wanted to meet her to get together, I asked her what worked for her.

The truth is, I didn't really care which restaurant my boyfriend and I went to and, because I determine my own working hours, I was able to be flexible time-wise with my friend. But over time, I discovered that my lack of preference had become a habit. I also realized that people began to conclude that my time was not as valuable as theirs. Unwittingly, I had broadcast a level of adaptability that had begun to chafe at me. Once I realized what was happening, I began stating a preference. And the more I did it, the more I realized that I actually *did* have a preference.

## Want Something? Say Something!

Sometimes, we know what we want and have to make sure we ask for it. Other times, it's in the talking itself that brings clarity.

Rebecca told me the following story. She had been married for ten years when she discovered her husband, Joel, was having an affair. When she confronted him, he told her that he wanted to keep seeing the other woman, but he didn't want to leave Rebecca. "I love you," he said.

She loved him, too, and couldn't imagine a life without him. Plus, she was terrified to live alone. They talked for a long time. He told her that after so many years, it was natural that certain aspects of their relationship had faded. He said it was a reasonable idea for him to meet some of his emotional and sexual needs with this other woman.

Rebecca thought about it. She didn't want to lose him and she wanted him to be happy. She wondered if she could accept this arrangement. Joel made it seem so reasonable. She wanted to be a reasonable person. She wanted to have liberated views. She decided to give it a try.

But as the weeks progressed, she felt sick most of the time and her anxiety became so debilitating that she had trouble sleeping. She was miserable.

Rebecca had not told anyone about what she was going through. "I didn't even tell my best friend," she said. "I felt embarrassed that I was afraid to be alone. Here I was, a strong, independent woman with a great life. I was ashamed that this was happening to me."

After a few months, she knew she needed help and made an appointment with a therapist. For the first time, she said out loud what was going on in her marriage and her life. She told me, "The second I said it out loud, I felt a burden come off my shoulders and I wondered why I would have thought this situation was okay."

After several months, she told Joel that she couldn't live with this situation anymore and told him he would need to move out. He was angry. He thought she was being unreasonable and tried to talk her into letting him stay.

"Prior to this experience," she told me, "I would have caved. I would have gone along with what he wanted. I would have agreed with him that I was being unreasonable, as he said it, 'to kick a man out of his own house.'"

Rebecca told me she had learned many valuable lessons

from this experience and was watchful of her tendency to automatically go along with what another person wanted. Now, when she is confronted with a situation about which she is unsure, she takes the time to figure out what she wants. She asks herself: Is this something I can get on board with? "I am better at saying no," she said.

"When I look back," she said, "I know that if I had shared what was going on with my close friends, instead of hiding because of shame and embarrassment, they would have helped me and I would have gotten clear about what I wanted earlier instead of later. Just saying it out loud to my therapist shifted everything. It was like I had been underwater and finally came to the surface. Once I told someone what I was going through, I knew what I wanted. It took me a few months to work through my feelings about my marriage and to be able to tell Joel what I wanted. But when I finally did speak to him, I didn't waver. He was unable to talk me into agreeing with him. I was strong. I was clear. I knew what I wanted."

## I Want to Go to the Ball!

When Cinderella finally asked for what she wanted, to go to a dance, she got more help than she could ever have dreamed of receiving. It took her a while to get there, to see beyond her situation, to envision a life that wasn't dedicated to catering to her stepmother and stepsisters. But get there, she did.

What I love about this story of wanting, asking, and receiving is that she didn't ask to be rescued from her situation, and she didn't ask her stepmother and stepsisters to agree with her. She didn't try to raise her self-esteem. She just asked for what she wanted. Very powerful! I love the miracle that manifested from her wish to go to the ball—a fairy godmother who showed up to help her.

Have you ever been in an ongoing difficult situation, perhaps in a relationship or job, and never created a vision for your future? Have you spent time and energy trying to convince others to agree with you and making their agreement a precondition for doing what you want? Or, have you given up thinking about what could make your life better and you happier?

## Here are some of the reasons you may not be asking for what you want:

- You are afraid of appearing selfish or greedy.
- You are afraid the answer will be no.
- You feel uncomfortable asking for something for yourself.
- You don't think your desires are important.
- You don't want others to know what you want.

- You are too focused on helping other people get what they want.

- You are afraid that asking for what you want will create conflict with people who are important to you.

When Cinderella asked to go to the ball, she simply asked for what she wanted. She didn't think about the logistics. She didn't analyze the probabilities. She didn't make it complicated. She could never have known ahead of time about the miracle that occurred and the impact it would have on her life. She just asked.

All of the fairy godmothers, people, and angels in the universe cannot help us if we don't want, ask, and then open up to receive their messages and assistance. Just like Cinderella, your life, too, will transform in miraculous ways once you give a voice to your dreams and desires.

## You Don't Get a Gold Star Just for Showing Up

I think most of us are past the gold-star philosophy, where you get a prize just for showing up. In the real world, people like what they see, or they don't. People are receptive to you, or they aren't. You must not only know what you want, you must prove yourself.

If you have a business, your job is to find out what the

public wants. If you want a relationship, you help yourself by being honest about your attractiveness to others—both internally and externally.

When I first tried to get an agent and publisher for my book *The Power of Receiving*, I could not get anyone interested. People were not receptive to a book about receiving! That unreceptive world made me reevaluate my manuscript. If I had not already been practicing receiving, I would have done what many people do—I would have tried harder. I would have done more. I would have given 500 percent.

But I had learned to pay attention when people are unreceptive. So, instead, I reevaluated how I was presenting an idea that was unfamiliar to most people. As a result, I explored my topic more deeply. From that exploration, I discovered that learning how to receive not only brings greater reciprocity to relationships, I found out that receptivity is also a powerful tool for helping people attract good things into their lives. I began giving workshops based on this new information and ultimately rewrote my book to include my new research. (I explain the story of this in *The Power of Receiving*.) After I finished writing my new manuscript, I wrote a query and a proposal, got an agent, and then a publisher, all within a short period of time. I finally had the right message. I had people's attention. I had a receptive world.

## Does What You Want, Want You?

I used to chase after my goals as if they were prey and I was the hunter. Whether I focused with laserlike intensity, wrote a detailed, grammatically correct wish list, or made bargains with God, I was a person who was *on task*. No halfhearted attempts from me!

When the goal-object of my affection didn't manifest— whether it was a desired writing project, a person, or some other goal, I would try to figure out what had gone wrong and what I could improve. Then, like Sisyphus rolling that boulder up the mountain, I would gather my energy for another try. It never occurred to me that this enormous expenditure of energy and effort was unnecessary. Only a 50 percent energy contribution was required from me to manifest my goal.

It's true that without initiative and activity, you will have a hard time accomplishing much of anything. But have you ever wondered what your goal wants from *you*? Like all partnerships, both members have to do their part. Life is a two-way street. If you think of your goal as checking *you* out to see if you are a good fit, it makes sense that being attractive to your goal is just as important as concentrating on what *you* want.

For example, no matter how much you want a particular

job, the people who are in charge of hiring must see you as someone they want. If you want to date a person who doesn't want to date you, you're out of luck.

Be receptive to the requirements and desires of others. The feedback you receive will help you know where to invest your energy and to make decisions based on what is actually going on instead of what you wish were going on.

Leave those boulder-rolling days behind you. Know that you are in charge of 50 percent and your goal has the other 50 percent. Ask your goal what it wants from you. Be a cooperative partner. If you are a high-maintenance person, your goal may think you are too much trouble and move on to someone else.

Wanting is a receptive power. Once you know what you want, you keep the energy moving by asking for it. Receiving the results of what you asked for is receptive. Doing something with those results is active. This is the circle of life. When you want without asking, you are interrupting this natural cycle. To reclaim your half of the universe: want, ask, and receive. These exercises will help you get there.

{ EXERCISES }

## 1. DON'T OBSESS ABOUT WHAT YOU *DON'T* WANT

Retrain your mind. When you find yourself thinking about what you *don't* want, replace those thoughts with what you *do* want. When you get a visual image of something that you don't want, create an image of you in the situation that you do want. Throughout the day, remind yourself about it.

## 2. SEND CINDERELLA TO REHAB

Find a quiet place where you can be alone. Fill three pages in a notebook or your journal. Write about what you want. Write quickly. Don't let your pen leave the page. Use the following format: *I want* [fill in the blank], *I want* [fill in the blank], *I want* [fill in the blank].

Keep the following in mind before you begin:

- Write about everything and anything you want. Don't limit yourself.
- Don't write about your desires for good things to happen for others. This is an exercise to help you discover what you want for *you*.

- Don't only write about the things you think you can easily accomplish.
- Write about desires that you keep secret. Write about the ones you are embarrassed about having. Include everything and you will clear out stuck energy.

Have fun! On the other side of this exercise is clarity.

## 3. CHOOSE WHAT YOU WANT

Be specific. Once you know what you want, you will be able to ask for it. You are not making a blood oath that you will be unable to undo. You are just choosing what you want in this moment. Don't make this exercise bigger or more complicated than it is.

This is what I want in my relationship:

_____

_____

This is what I want in my job:

_____

_____

This is what I want for my future:

_____

_____

This is what I want in my home:

_____

_____

This is what I want for my health:

_____

_____

This is what I want for the world:

_____

_____

This is what I want for today:

_____

_____

## 4. SAY WHAT YOU WANT

Let people know what you want. Don't ask only for those things that you think others will agree with. Ask for exactly what you want. People will either agree with you or they won't. People will either support you or they won't. The truth is that there are people who would help you if they only knew what it was that you wanted. Give them that gift.

## 5. WRITE DOWN WHAT YOU WANT

Start with one goal and give it your undivided attention. Give it a completion date so that you can evaluate whether or not you reached your goal.

My goal is to _____

_____

by _____

_____

(date).

### { INSPIRING QUOTES }

*Burning desire to be or do something gives us
staying power—a reason to get up every
morning or to pick ourselves up and start
in again after a disappointment.*

∘ MARSHA SINETAR ∘

*A lot of people are afraid to say what they want.
That's why they don't get what they want.*

∘ MADONNA ∘

*Desire makes life happen. Makes it matter.*
*Makes everything worth it. Desire is life.*
*Hunger to see the next sunrise or sunset,*
*to touch the one you love, to try again.*

∘ KAREN MARIE MONING ∘

*Most people are so busy knocking themselves out,*
*trying to do everything they think they should do,*
*they never get around to do what they want to do.*

∘ KATHLEEN WINSOR ∘

*The voice of our original self is often muffled,*
*overwhelmed, even strangled, by the voices*
*of other people's expectations.*

∘ JULIA CAMERON ∘

*Ask for what you want and be prepared to get it!*

∘ MAYA ANGELOU ∘

*When your heart speaks, take good notes.*

∘ JUDITH CAMPBELL ∘

{ Step Three }

# Ask for Help If You Need It and Accept It When It's Offered

Do you ask for help only after you have exhausted what you can do by yourself? You are not alone. In our pull-yourself-up-by-your-bootstraps society, asking for help is, for many people, a last-resort option. Yet, while you may feel it is undignified to ask a fellow human being for help, do you feel perfectly comfortable asking God, the Universe, or a Higher Power for help?

Perhaps we should designate one day of the week as "Ask a Mortal Day" so that we remember that we are all in this together and that being helped is as natural and as important as helping others.

The reality is that people perform tasks that help you every day. They pour your coffee, bag your groceries, give inspiring sermons, educate you, cook your meals, sew the clothes you wear, and make the products you use, to name only a few. But sometimes you need to ask for what you need or want because others don't anticipate your needs, or they don't know how to help, or they don't want to help.

Reluctance to ask for what you want contaminates your ability to give. This is because the giver and the receiver are a team. Every act of giving has a recipient—the person who receives what is given. When one member of the team is not healthy, the other is not either.

When you think about it, how do you really think about the person you are helping if you have such a dim opinion about being helped yourself? And why do so many of us look the other way when we walk past people in obvious need and call the individual who stops to help a hero?

A culture that grants a halo to a giver while denying equal respect to the receiver (who made the giving possible) can't help but have a deleterious effect on government programs, community groups, and charities.

We call programs that help people "entitlement" programs but are ambivalent about how much recipients are entitled to. Many charitable organizations are inept at utilizing volunteers. People who work in the helping professions are some of the lowest-paid members of our workforce.

The reality is that everybody at some time will be in a situation where they need help, whether due to a natural disaster, an illness, or a loss of mobility due to aging, or for countless other reasons. It's a shame that in addition to needing help, people are distressed by having to rely on someone other than themselves. They are twice traumatized—first by needing help and then by receiving it.

## Bad Breath, a Dead Fish, and a Curious Dolphin

*Lola the Whale*, a charming children's story by Pedro Pablo Sacristán Sanz, illustrates the consequences and the absurdity of refusing to ask for help.

In this story, Lola is so embarrassed by her bad breath, which is caused by a small dead fish trapped in her mouth, that she avoids everyone. She tries repeatedly, but unsuccessfully, to dislodge the stinky culprit.

Lola is lonely and others are beginning to think that she is a snob because she doesn't want to hang out with them anymore. Dido, a curious dolphin, follows her, sees that she is trying to get something out of her mouth, and realizes the source of her trouble.

When Dido realized this, she offered to help, but Lola didn't want to bother her with her bad breath. Nor did she want anyone to find out.

"I don't want them to think I have bad breath," said Lola.

"Is that why you've spent so much time away from everyone?" answered Dido, unable to believe it. "They don't think you've got bad breath, they think you're unpleasant, boring, and ungrateful, and that you hate everyone. Do you think that's better?"

Lola realized that her pride—her exaggerated shyness, and not letting anyone help—had created an even greater problem. Full of regret, she asked Dido to remove the remains of the fish in her mouth.

When this was done, Lola began speaking to everyone again. However, she had to make a big effort to be accepted again by her friends. Lola decided that never again would she fail to ask for help when she really needed it.*

I doubt if you've ever had to deal with a dead fish stuck in your mouth, but have you tried any of the following without any support or help?

---

* The full text for *Lola the Whale* can be found at:
freestoriesforkids.com/children/stories-and-tales/lola-whale.

- Eat healthier food
- Start exercising
- Stop drinking
- Save money
- Make money
- Find a mate
- Leave a relationship
- Figure out what you want to do with your life
- Write a book
- Find a job
- Leave a job
- Sell your house
- Buy a house

Do you feel like a failure if you are unable to reach your goal by yourself? What have you done to increase your chances of success? How many people, groups, or associations have you asked for help?

## Here are some of the reasons why you may decide not to ask for help:

- You feel that wanting something for yourself is selfish.
- You feel that you shouldn't burden others with your problems.

- You believe that people who get what they want without help are admirable.

- You believe that those who achieve success while enduring significant hardships are even more admirable.

Aren't you frustrated, however, when *you* are the one who wants to help someone and they refuse to let you?

Even though our culture is infatuated with a person who does it all, carrying 100 percent of the load is not natural and is not the behavior of an empowered woman. The reality is that a woman who takes on too much pays a high price for this unrealistic, foolish endeavor.

When you ask for and accept help, you strengthen your receptive powers by inviting energy to come toward you. And that makes you a magnet for receiving ideas, people, gifts, and countless other goodies. This balances your giving—when energy is moving outward.

By both giving and receiving, you allow a metaphorical gate to swing both ways. Sometimes it opens away from you and sometimes toward you. If you have a gate that only goes only one way—away from you—you will drain every last bit of your energy. That is neither empowering nor helping you or anybody else.

## How to Ask For Help

Here are ideas that will help you get into the habit of asking:

- Don't wait for someone to offer help if you need it now.

- Don't complain about what you are not getting. Ask for what you need.

- Be specific. Don't make people guess.

- If people do not help you, don't give up after you ask. Use your staying power.

- Be grateful when people help you. Don't take them for granted.

- Say thank you after someone helps you.

- Reciprocate if it feels right to you, and don't return the favor if it doesn't. You can always pay it forward and help someone else.

When you ask for help, sometimes the answer will be yes, sometimes the answer will be no, and sometimes you will need to compromise and negotiate. The point is to get used to asking for help—not to get everything you want.

## Whom to Ask for Help

- Your mate
- Your children
- A coworker
- An employee
- Your boss
- A friend
- A neighbor
- A sibling

## Where Do You Need Help?

- Are you caring for a parent or ill family member?
- Do you need a plan for help with child care?
- Are you overwhelmed at work and need help from a coworker?
- Are family members helping with household chores?

# Maria's Story

Maria needed help when Hurricane Sandy flooded her Long Island home and her car floated away. Her home office on the ground floor was uninhabitable and all of her papers and office equipment were ruined, along with everything else on the first floor and in the basement. She had no heat or electricity, and she and her young daughter were taken in by her brother and his family.

Maria told me she was getting a big lesson in receiving. She said, "Within days of my personal devastation, friends, colleagues, students, and clients began to reach out. At first I was in a 'Thank you, but no thank you' mode and told them to kindly direct their donations to hurricane victims worse off than myself. I was sure I'd be fine.

"They didn't listen. In fact, I was told that people wanted to help me because they knew me. They felt that helping someone they felt a personal connection to was more meaningful than an anonymous donation they wouldn't be able to track. I was honored. It wasn't until I had a conversation with one of my friends that I realized it was my turn to accept help.

"She said, 'Maria, you know better than anyone else that everything happens in cycles. There are times when you're up, and during those times it's your responsibility to help someone who is down. But when it's you experiencing a downturn, that's when it's your responsibility to allow others to help lift you up.'

"My friend's words helped me move out of my own way, and I graciously began to accept the financial help offered."

# Liz's Story

Liz frequently has to confront the issue of how, when, and where to ask for help due to her disability. She told me the following story:

"When I go to the grocery store and I am in my wheelchair, it is not easy to get the items out of my shopping basket and put them on the conveyer belt at the checkout counter. I used to refuse to let people help me because I felt that it was important for me to do it by myself.

"One day, after I had been reading your book [*The Power of Receiving*], I was in line at the grocery store and a woman asked me if she could put my items on the conveyor belt for me. I almost told her, 'Thank you, but no.' But then I thought about what you said in your book, that receiving is just as important as giving. I thanked her and told her that I would love the help. We had a lovely chat as we were waiting in line. I felt great about the whole experience and regret that I had not learned to receive before this. It seems so silly now when I think about how many times I refused to let people help me. Now if I need help, I ask, and I say yes when people offer."

## Leymah Gbowee's story

Leymah Gbowee, a Liberian woman living through her country's civil war under the brutal dictator Charles Taylor, wanted peace. To achieve her goal, she needed help and sought advice and training from women and men who lived in other African countries and who had experience in peace movements.

Under Gbowee's leadership, Muslim and Christian women joined together and employed a variety of receptive methods, including peaceful protests, sit-ins, and inclusion— inviting people to participate in the cause. They even went on a sex strike, refusing to have sex with their husbands until the men helped them achieve peace. This tactic brought needed media attention.

The women's peace movement eventually brought an end to the civil war and an end to Charles Taylor's tyrannical reign. Gbowee's efforts paved the way for Ellen Johnson Sirleaf to be elected as Liberia's first female president. President Sirleaf and Leymah Gbowee were awarded the Nobel Peace Prize in 2011.

You may think that you, too, would ask for help if you were building a peace movement or trying to overthrow a dictator. But are you involved in institutions with much less at stake? Are you a member of a board, committee, group, organization, or family, and are doing most of the work?

The truth is that the person in charge is often resented as well as unappreciated by others because of the concentration of power that is in that one person's hands. The word "delegate" is most often used when we ask people to stop doing it all. But really what we are saying is to ask for help.

## Obligation: If I Accept the Help, Do I Owe the Helper?

The issue of obligation is one of the most asked-about questions I receive from women. Many women turn away offers of help because they fear they will have to do something they don't want to do as a result of accepting help. Men do not, as a general rule, have the same fear.

The truth is that accepting help never obligates you. You do not erase your ability to set boundaries exactly where you need them to be. But when you don't have experience, it's hard to know how to handle these situations.

Esther contacted me after reading my first book, *The Power of Receiving*, and told me the following story:

She had fallen in love with a man who, although he enjoyed being intimate with her, was honest that he did not see her as a potential partner. "We were kind of like a couple but with no commitments," she told me. She stayed with him for several months until he returned to an ex-girlfriend.

Esther had recently lost her job and this same man wanted to help her find a new job and gave her a contact number for a person who could potentially hire her.

"I said I did not need his help. I feel like he is paying me back a favor for all the help I gave him when his life was a mess. I have a terrible conflict because I am a single mom and I need a job, but I honestly don't want to owe him anything. I honestly need to forget him, and I feel that by accepting this favor I would never be able to move on. I also feel he is helping me because he feels sorry for how I feel now. I don't know what to do. I don't want to have too much pride. I need a job."

It's okay for this man to feel sorry for Esther and about what happened. That does not take away any of her dignity. Maybe it's the right thing for him to feel bad. Maybe it's the right thing for him to help her.

Have you ever turned away help that would improve your life for any of the following reasons?

- Because of pride
- Because of the person who is offering
- Because of fear of obligation
- Because you think you should handle the situation by yourself

Maria, the Sandy storm victim, initially felt guilty about accepting help from her friends and clients who sent her money after she suffered losses from the hurricane.

"I found it interesting that I first went through a cycle of grace, accepting the help, but as soon as I started using the money for my recovery, I felt tremendous guilt and felt like I owed the people who helped me. I found it interesting how my gut reaction to accepting help was to immediately offer something so I didn't feel like the people who helped me had 'one up on me.' Does that make any sense?"

When guilt prompts you to reciprocate, the giving is tainted. You don't feel happy. Instead, you are consumed with regret about the whole situation—both the receiving and the giving parts.

The following story is about a woman asking for help and then wondering if she was obligated to accept the help that was offered, even though it wasn't what she wanted:

Emily worked at a demanding job, and by the time she returned home each evening to her unemployed husband and teenage son, she was exhausted. Her requests for help with the laundry and cooking were met with unenthusiastic and only periodic compliance. When I asked her what they said when she asked for help, she told me that although they promised to help, they only occasionally pitched in. When they did help, they mixed the clothes together so that the white clothes got dingy. They were careless about what went into the dryer, so certain clothes shrank or were ruined. And their idea of "helping" with dinner was to order take-out food.

Emily felt stymied by their lackadaisical attitude and their carelessness. What would have helped Emily? Not giving up, the willingness to face conflict, and honoring her feelings. But she did what many women do—she caved.

## Earth Angels, Heavenly Beings, and Your Prayers

When you pray, you are asking for help. Asking God, angels, relatives who have crossed over, various spirits, and nature sprites for help has been going on for eons, according to what we know from recorded history. While we may not use some of their methods such as human and animal sacrifices, we do light candles, create vision boards, and count rosaries or mala beads, among other methods. We beseech those on the other side to do what they can to help us.

It's comforting to be looked after, to know that we matter, and that we can receive help from the other side, through divine intervention. And there are countless studies that demonstrate the positive results of prayer.

Asking for help is even supported by religious texts, as in the following passage from the Bible, in Luke 11:9.

*And I say unto you, Ask, and it shall be given you; seek,*
*and ye shall find; knock, and it shall be opened unto you.*

I'll tell you a story from my own life. A few years ago, I moved from the East Coast to Arizona. Soon after I arrived, I asked God, the Universe, and crossed-over relatives to send me a sign that I was being watched over. That evening, I went to the grocery store and when I was returning to my car with my groceries, I saw someone putting something on the windshield. It was dark, so I couldn't see clearly. But once I got there, I saw a note with a dollar bill. A short distance away, I saw three little girls and their mother watching me.

The note, written on a torn piece of envelope, read, "This is for you because Jesus *loves* you." Now, I am not a religious person, preferring nature's cathedral to organized religion. But I welcome any message that is loving and kind.

"Did you leave this wonderful message for me with the dollar bill?" I asked them. Yes, they had, they told me.

"You are angels!" I said. "I recently moved to Arizona and I asked God today to send me a sign that I was being watched over. Thank you so much. I feel so welcomed in my new home state of Arizona!"

All three girls rushed over and hugged me and one of

them gave me another dollar bill. "We picked your car out of all the cars in the parking lot!" one of the girls said.

I was quite overcome. "I will never forget you," I told them.

Five years later, the note and the two dollar bills are held to my refrigerator by a magnet—a reminder of the magic that occurs simply by asking.

## An Organization that Refused Help from Volunteers

I used to volunteer for a nonprofit organization. I stopped volunteering because I was exhausted by the staff's refusal to accept my help. I also stopped bringing friends to this organization because their skills were not utilized and they also were turned away.

One day, a friend and I brought numerous garbage bags filled with donations. A staff person showed us the room where we could leave it. In that room was a jumble of items. My friend and I offered to sort through and organize not only the bags we had brought, but also the other things. The women said, "No, don't worry about it. We'll take care of it later." Knowing how short-staffed they were, I said, "We are happy to help, and really, we have nowhere else to be." "No," she said. "We'll just take care of it later."

I was mystified by her refusal. I asked her if she would

have to remain with us if we were to stay and organize the donations. No, she didn't have to remain with us. My friend and I gave up and left. This was the same friend who had generously offered her expertise and skills in an area they desperately needed. My friend never went back. And I followed her example soon after.

We want life to give to us, but we turn the gift away when it shows up!

## Ask for What You Need

When I told a neighbor that I was writing a chapter about asking for and accepting help, she said, "Make sure you tell your readers that they need to be specific about what they need." She had just emerged from a year of debilitating health problems that had caused her to rely on others. She knew firsthand how well-intentioned people can give in a way that is not helpful at all. She also knew how people may not offer to help because they don't know what to do.

This also occurs in the distribution of aid after a disaster. After Hurricane Sandy, I read about towns that had received donated items that they didn't need and not enough of what they did need.

Often, people feel so grateful that they are getting help at all that they don't want to appear ungrateful by saying that what is being given is not needed.

Every act of giving has a receiver, a caregiver has a care-receiver, and how the receivers handle their part is just as important as how the giver gives.

Here is an example: Ellen, an elderly woman, lived by herself. After an operation, she needed help with house-work, shopping, walking her dog, and getting to and from her medical appointments. Because she felt embarrassed to ask for help, her dog didn't get needed walks, her house didn't get cleaned, and she didn't have the food that would have helped in her recovery. Although family members were available to transport her to rehab, she arranged for a van service to take her.

She could have had a list for all of these activities, since children and grandchildren were nearby. But she didn't want to ask. I have a motto: The only possible match for someone who doesn't know how to receive is someone who doesn't know how to give. In Ellen's case, it did not occur to her child and grandchildren, who lived less than a mile away, to help her, since they were used to being on the receiving rather than the giving end of their relationship with her.

How could she have handled her recovery period? She could have written a list of the things that needed to be done and asked for help from the people to whom she had given so much.

Imagine if the Red Cross and other relief agencies, as well as individuals, had the equivalent of a wedding registry, where people could list the things that would most help them. When we provide avenues for receivers to express their specific needs, we honor the receivers and make them equal to the givers.

## Don't Make People Guess

A lack of specificity easily creates misunderstandings, as in the following stories:

Debra was frequently frustrated by her employees until she learned to stop being indirect. She used to ask them to show up early for an event, instead of saying, "Be there at 8:45 A.M." Then she would be upset when they were late. She would ask her employees to wear dress-up shoes instead of black shoes and discover one of them wore his dress-up sneakers! She asked her employees to wear a white shirt, and one of her new female employees showed up for work wearing her husband's shirt, which was several sizes too big. The employees ended up feeling picked on and unappreciated, and Debra felt frustrated.

Here is another example: Bobbi, a new mother, told her husband that she needed more help from him. But he did not know exactly what she needed and so his help was unappreciated since it didn't meet her needs. She felt guilty because she loved him and he was a wonderful father and husband, and she didn't want to sound like a harpy. But her vagueness caused problems. Once she asked for exactly what she needed, everyone was happier.

The active and receptive are a team. All kinds of difficulties are caused by disrupting that connection. Many women are too busy and exhausted to reclaim their half of the universe, further contributing to the imbalances in our society, in relationships, and in themselves.

If you are habitually giving more than 50 percent, you are doing too much. Reclaim your half of the universe. Ask for help when you need it and accept it when it's offered, and you will give yourself energy, good health, and a happier life.

These exercises will pave the way.

## { EXERCISES }

### 1. "ASK A MORTAL DAY"

Designate one day each week to ask people for help, whether you need someone to help you sort through a problem, need help finding a job, or would love to learn a new recipe. Here are examples:

Today I will ask a friend for help with:

_____

_____

Today I will ask a coworker to help me:

_____

_____

Today I will ask my children to:

_____

_____

Today I will ask my spouse for help with:

_____

_____

## 2. NOTICE AND ACKNOWLEDGE THE PEOPLE WHO HELP YOU EVERY DAY

Don't spend your days on autopilot. Who is performing tasks for you? Is it the person who bags your groceries, the server who refills your coffee, or a coworker who offers to help you with a work project? Notice them. Say something. Smile!

### 3. ALLOW PEOPLE TO RECIPROCATE

When the giver and receiver relate to each other, the energy keeps moving. If you do something for someone and she wants to return the favor, let her.

### 4. MAKE A LIST OF THE PEOPLE FROM WHOM YOU WOULD LIKE HELP

Don't try to carry 100 percent of the load. If you are habitually carrying more than 50 percent, you are doing too much. Dial it back! The people in your life are there to help you. Who are they?

### 5. ASK FOR EXACTLY WHAT YOU NEED

Don't make people guess. Be specific. If you are not sure about what you need, take the time to figure it out before you say anything. General statements frequently cause misunderstandings.

## { INSPIRING QUOTES }

*We need to compose our lives in such a way
that we both give and receive, learning
to do both with grace.*

○ MARY CATHERINE BATESON ○

*Trouble is a part of your life and if you don't
share it, you don't give the person who loves
you a chance to love you enough.*

○ DINAH SHORE ○

*When we give cheerfully and
accept gratefully, everyone is blessed.*

○ MAYA ANGELOU ○

*Asking for help does not mean that we are weak
or incompetent. It usually indicates an advanced
level of honesty and intelligence.*

○ ANNE WILSON SCHAEF ○

*Why push yourself to your breaking point when
there are people who would be honored
to help lighten your load?*

○ LORI DESCHENE ○

> *The strong individual is the one who asks*
> *for help when [s]he needs it.*
>
> ◦ RONA BARRETT ◦

> *Courage starts with showing up and*
> *letting ourselves be seen.*
>
> ◦ BRENÉ BROWN ◦

# Be Grateful and Say Thank You

When I was a kid, I was taught to say thank you when someone said something complimentary, told to write thank-you letters to the people who had given me a gift, and to say a blessing before a meal.

It seems so simple: Say thank you when someone has done something nice for you. When did gratitude become complicated, something to be worked on, something to analyze so deeply? Numerous books have been devoted to this subject, research projects have investigated the benefits of expressing gratitude, and websites and blogs are intent on reminding us to feel grateful.

And now, here I am devoting a whole chapter to

the subject of gratitude and even telling you that it is one of seven steps that will help you reclaim your half of the universe. Could there be anything more to add to this topic? Keep reading.

Gratitude, in the way that I am talking about it as a receptive power, is synonymous with being appreciative, noticing, and being aware of your surroundings. Energy moves toward you as you take in and receive what is going on around you and in you.

Gratitude has such power because it causes you to be present. When you are present, your five senses open and you hear, touch, see, taste, and smell your environment.

When you get used to noticing what is in your environment, you begin appreciating the sounds, textures, sights, tastes, aromas, and the kindnesses that people extend to you. These experiences fill you up and become a power in your life. It's like you have plugged into your life instead of barreling through it. Here are examples:

- When you say thank you to the person who bags your groceries, you are not just saying it, you acknowledge that particular individual who has just done you a service.

- When you see a beautiful flower, you don't just glance at it, you admire it.

- When you drink your morning coffee, you don't chug it down, you fully experience the taste and aroma.

- When you hear birds chirping, they are not background noise, you pay attention to the sound they make.

## Be Where You Are

If you are busy and distracted, you are not grateful because you are not present. You don't notice anything. You are inside your head, ten steps ahead of what you are doing, or you are ruminating about something from the past. Doesn't it make sense that you have to notice something to appreciate it?

Many people who have attended my classes or workshops don't have trouble with the gratitude exercise when I ask them to make a list of everything for which they feel grateful. They are poised to write their list but stop when I add: "everything you are grateful for since you woke up this morning."

It's not that they are ungrateful people—it's just that they are not used to being grateful as a way of moving through the world, of observing the world. They had not thought to notice their environment that morning.

# Ingratitude Equals Neglect

What happens when you don't pay attention, listen, acknowledge, notice, or receive someone? They notice your lack of attention—and they don't like it! Psychologists report that when parents are indifferent to their child, that indifference is worse than treating the child poorly. Not mattering is worse.

This idea applies to your everyday experiences, too. Have you ever witnessed someone being rude to a waiter—acting as if the person taking their order is not a fellow human being? Servers who are unacknowledged and unappreciated notice that treatment. How could they not?

Have you ever been treated by people as being insignificant—like you are the least important person in the room? It doesn't feel good. So much relationship strife is due to people feeling unacknowledged, unappreciated, unimportant, and taken for granted. Inanimate objects, plants, and animals also show the effects of ingratitude and neglect.

## Here are some of the consequences of this negligence:

- People see you as rude, uncaring, and worse.
- Children feel unloved.

- Parents feel taken for granted.

- Employees feel unappreciated.

- Bosses feel unappreciated.

- Teachers are frustrated.

- Students don't learn.

- Animals suffer.

- Plants die.

- Your living space is a mess.

- Your car has trash in it.

- The air, water, and earth are polluted.

## Recharge Your Battery

Being appreciative is a way to gain energy. It connects you with a power source. Every time you connect, you are recharged. Every time you disconnect, you drain your energy, your battery.

You already know that you need sleep to recharge. Think of receiving what is going on around you and recognizing the value of what is in your environment as doing the same thing. Appreciation opens your sense receptors and life-energy flows into you through them.

Think of how energized and full you feel
in the following situations:

- When you watch a colorful sunset
- When you spend time with people who care
  about you
- When you see someone doing a good deed
- When you hear a funny joke
- When you listen to beautiful music
- When you spend time with your pet
- When you receive a kiss from someone you love
- When you taste a favorite food

## Your Appreciation Counts

The more you appreciate, notice, and acknowledge the people, animals, plants, and objects in your environment, the
more receptive power you have. Fortunately, you have numerous opportunities every day to think, write, say, and
express your appreciation.

### Silent Gratitude

You may have heard the saying that a butterfly that flaps its
wings in South America can cause a typhoon in Japan. Energy expenditure has a ripple effect. An easy way to think

about this is to imagine being in a pool, walking through the water. You can feel the water on your body as you displace the water as you walk. If you wave your hand through the air, you can feel the air against your skin as you displace the air. Your thoughts and feelings also move energy.

Here is an example: You see someone with a great haircut and you think: *That woman's hair looks great.* But you don't say it out loud. You might not tell the woman because you believe that, for example, interrupting her conversation is not the appropriate thing to do at that time. Maybe you are walking down the street and you don't know the woman with the fabulous haircut. But your appreciation still counts because your thought creates a ripple effect.

Here is another example: You hear beautiful music and you think, *What a great song! Those musicians are amazing!* You don't say it out loud because you are at the symphony, or perhaps you are alone listening to the radio in your car. But, again, your appreciation still counts.

What might you be doing instead of enjoying the music or admiring the hair? You could be draining your cell phone battery by texting while walking (or worse, texting while driving). You could be talking on your cell phone when you are out with your children. Or, you could be thinking about the day you just went through or the evening coming up, instead of noticing where you are and the sights and sounds that surround you.

## Writing Gratitude

When you write down your gratitude, you make a greater commitment. Many people write regularly in a gratitude journal. Research has demonstrated the positive results of maintaining a regular gratitude practice.

The power of written gratitudes is not lessened or strengthened by where or when you write them. You may want to start your day writing in your gratitude journal.* Or you may want to write your gratitudes before you go to sleep. You can write them on the back of a receipt in your car while waiting at a red light or on a napkin at a restaurant.

A thank-you letter expressing your appreciation for a gift, good deed, or anything else you were delighted to receive is a way of giving back to the person who gave to you. You can write your appreciation in a card, letter, email, or text. Depending on the generation, different forms will be more meaningful than others to the recipient.

### Here are examples:

- Write in a journal anything for which you are grateful.
- Write a thank-you letter to the person who has given you a gift or has helped you in some way.

---

* Go to www.AmandaOwen.com for information about *The Power of Receiving Journal*.

- Write a review online for an author about a book that you enjoyed.

- Comment on Facebook when you appreciate the message.

- Send birthday and holiday cards to those you love.

- Send a thank-you card to someone who has written a recommendation for you.

- Write a congratulations note to someone who has achieved a goal.

- Email your public officials when they vote for legislation that is important to you.

## The Power of a Thank-You Letter

Gerda Lerner, among her numerous accomplishments, created the first graduate program in women's history in the United States, established a doctoral program in women's history at the University of Wisconsin, and wrote several textbooks on women's history.

In an article highlighting Gerda Lerner's achievements, Dinesh Ramde, a journalist for the Associated Press, reported that Gerda's daughter, Stephanie Lerner, still remembered a former student who wrote to her mother thirty years after taking her classes, saying that no one had been more influential in her life. Stephanie said, "The student wrote, 'I thought you were impossible, difficult, not understanding, but you gave me a model of commitment that I've never had before.'"

The daughter of a woman who had accomplished so much still remembered that thank-you letter, which was written all those years ago.

## Teaching Gratitude

Unfortunately, thank-you cards seem to be a relic of the past. It used to be mandatory for children, after receiving a gift, to get out the crayons and paper to make thank-you drawings for Grandma and Grandpa. These days, when I talk about gratitude during my workshops, people seek me out to talk about their disappointment that their grandchildren don't send thank-you cards even though they had taught their own children to make drawings and, when older, to write a thank-you letter.

Do you ever complain to others about this lack of gratitude and breach of social etiquette, but never bring up the subject with the parents of the children? You are not alone.

By the time a friend of mine had spent fifteen years putting money into a bank account for her only granddaughter's college education, she had quite a bit of money saved.

But after never receiving thank-you letters or calls for the gifts she had sent through the years, she reallocated those funds and donated them to an organization whose cause she supported. Since she had never told anybody that she had saved all of that money, when she changed her mind, no one was the wiser.

## Why is this very common situation so hard to talk about?

- Fear of conflict
- Worry that you may be seen as meddling
- Feeling vulnerable about saying you would like to be acknowledged and appreciated
- Not wanting to keep harping on it if you've already mentioned it
- A culture that tells us that it's not true giving if you care about being thanked for something you have given (as if the giver and receiver are not at all related!)

When I told a friend that I was writing about this subject, she confided that she was upset that she had never received a thank-you letter or an acknowledgment of any kind from her niece, a young woman about whom she cared deeply. She had never said a word to her niece about how she felt.

After our conversation, she wrote a letter to her niece about her feelings, who promptly called her the moment she received it. They talked on the phone for a long time. It had never occurred to her niece that her lack of acknowledgment had hurt her favorite aunt. By the time the conversation was over, they were closer than they had ever been. My friend's willingness to face her fears and feelings of vulnerability had given her a wonderful gift.

Some years ago, I was in the same situation. After years of giving gifts, cash, and gift cards to my nieces and nephew, and never receiving a thank-you card, letter, note, drawing, email, or text, I sent the following to two of my nieces and one nephew whose birthdays fell within days of one another.

I sent cash along with a self-addressed stamped envelope and a survey questionnaire. Feel free to copy and use it.

I received the self-addressed stamped envelope back with wonderful comments and thanks from my nieces and nephew, along with their apologies for not having expressed their gratitude sooner.

Dear _____ ,

Happy Birthday! I thought I would make it easier this year for you to thank me for your birthday gift. I have enclosed a self-addressed, stamped envelope and a form (below) where you can check the appropriate boxes. I have also left space in case you want to write your own message. I am enclosing $___ in this envelope. I hope you will spend it on something you enjoy. With that said—onward! Following is the form. Check all that apply.

---------------------------- *CUT HERE* ----------------------------

☐　Thanks for the money!

☐　I really appreciate it that you remember my birthday each year!

☐　I plan on spending the money on (fill in here)

_____

☐　Even though I am not going to call, email, or write to thank you, I would really appreciate it if you continue to send me something each year for my birthday!

☐　Please stop sending me birthday cards or anything else! It's annoying!

Please use the space below if you would like to add a personal note.

## Saying Gratitude

How something is received is just as important as how it is given. When you tell someone you have appreciated something they have given to you, whether it is a gift, compliment, help, or anything else, you are giving a gift to them.

An elementary school teacher, who had taken my five-week course that teaches people how to achieve their goals by learning how to receive, shared with me how learning to receive had changed the way she had her students do a particular exercise.

She told me that prior to taking my course, one of her favorite exercises was to have her students stand in a circle while each child said something they liked about each member of the group. It had never occurred to her that how a person responded to a compliment was just as important as giving it. After taking my course, she told me, she would teach her students this valuable lesson and ask the child receiving the compliment to say thank you.

### Here are examples of situations to express your gratitude out loud:

- Say thank you to a server who refills your coffee.
- Say thank you to the person who bags your groceries.
- Say thank you to a teacher for educating your child.

- Say "thank you for your service" to a person who is a member of the military.

- Say a blessing before a meal.

## Showing Gratitude

The sayings "walk your talk" and "actions speak louder than words" describe the heft, the weight of doing something. It counts in a way that thoughts and words don't. I remember easily, and will for the rest of my life, the times when people went out of their way to help me.

### Here are examples of how you can show your gratitude:

- Take someone out to dinner to show your appreciation for something they did for you.

- Bring a gift from your travels for the person who picks you up from the airport.

- Deliver food to a friend who is ill.

- Sign up for a charity walk.

- Volunteer for a cause you support.

- Spend time with someone who is in the hospital.

- Mentor a young person.

- Offer to babysit for a busy single mother.

- Attend a memorial service of a person you admire.

- Pick up litter.

- Recycle.
- Plant a tree.
- Pay it forward.

Rachel Carson, a scientist and writer, is often credited with beginning the environmental movement. She wrote about the natural world and taught people to appreciate its beauty. She later famously turned her attention to the use of chemical pesticides and wrote about it in her book *Silent Spring*. Rachel Carson's body of work is a kind of thank-you letter to Earth.

## The Gratitude Bank

There are two ways to make a gratitude deposit: time and energy.

We use the word "appreciate" to say that something has increased in value. Think of your appreciation as making gratitude deposits. Each time you appreciate something, whether you think, write, say, or show it, your value goes up, your energy increases, and your receptive power strengthens. You, your life, those with whom you come into contact, Earth—everybody and everything benefits.

Many studies have shown that the more grateful you are, the more you have to be grateful for. It multiplies. So the more grateful you are, the more energy you have, the happier you are, and the more you make a positive influence on those you know, and even strangers.

You can express your appreciation in any number of ways. You can spend a lot of time on some forms and less time on others. Here are examples:

- You can write your gratitudes every day.
- You can think grateful thoughts throughout the day.
- You can say thank you to people.
- You can say a blessing before a meal.
- You can give the gift of listening to the person who is talking.
- You can throw a ball for your dog.
- You can write a thank-you note.
- You can buy a gift for the person who picks you up from the airport.
- You can bring food to a friend who is home sick.
- You can take care of the things you own.

## These are examples of the things for which you can be grateful:

- I am grateful for my morning coffee.
- I am grateful for the singing birds.

- I am grateful that my mother is feeling better.
- I am grateful that I found a gifted massage therapist.
- I am grateful that my friend found a job.
- I am grateful for my beautiful home.
- I am grateful that I exercised yesterday.

Do you get the idea that you can never run out of things to be grateful for?

Many people are grateful only for the things that make them happy. But gratefulness is not a synonym for happiness. Gratitude is an expression of appreciation, which is not the same as happiness. I am sure you can think of an instance that did not make you happy, but for which you were still grateful.

Make a point to not only be grateful for your more virtuous qualities and fun experiences, but also to be grateful for your wholeness, which includes experiences that are uncomfortable or even painful. You can include feelings and observations such as these:

- I am grateful I am able to feel my grief.
- I am grateful that I am aware of the shortcomings I need to change within myself.
- I am grateful I was able to leave a destructive relationship.

You can vary the way you express your gratitude. Here are variations for "I am grateful" or "thank you":

- I appreciate
- I feel blessed
- I recognize
- I acknowledge
- I give credit
- I respect
- I admire
- I am in awe

## The Receptive Power of Gratitude

Gratitude is so highly valued these days that it almost seems like a moral failing to feel ungrateful. But too often people use the words "gratitude" and "happiness" as synonyms. Have you ever been told to feel grateful when you are feeling depressed? How irritating is it when people want you to tie a big, happy pink bow around something that is causing you misery?

When I was growing up, the word "Pollyanna" (a girl from a book and movie) was used to describe someone who is so cheerful and optimistic, a glass-*always*-half-full person, that his or her positivity made you want to throw up or give that person something to be depressed about.

Living a receptive life is about being true to yourself. It's about honesty and integrity. It is also about inclusion, which means that you welcome all feelings, not just the happy ones and not just the sad ones.

Be grateful for experiences that are lovely, heart-warming, kind, and beautiful. But don't ignore your feelings or pretend that difficulties do not exist. Don't be overly selective about what you choose to appreciate.

The miracle that occurs after practicing gratitude over a period of time is that the things and experiences for which you feel grateful shift and change. And that in itself leads you to some very rich, powerful, and interesting dimensions within yourself and in your life.

To reclaim your half of the universe, be grateful and say "Thank you." These exercises will help you get there.

## { EXERCISES }

### 1. PAY ATTENTION

Be attentive as you move through your day. What do you hear, see, taste, smell, and touch?

Do you hear traffic, the hum of a fan, or your cat's purr?

Do you see the colorful clothes that people are wearing?

Do you taste the food you eat?

Do you smell the aroma of your morning coffee?

Do you feel the fabric of a shirt as you put it on?

### 2. ACKNOWLEDGE PEOPLE

Don't treat people you encounter as if they are insignificant.

Wave your thanks to the person who lets you go first at a stop sign or merge into traffic.

Don't talk on your cell phone when you are in the middle of a transaction or a conversation.

Notice the grocery clerk who is ringing up your order.

Make eye contact with the waiter who hands you a menu.

## 3. WRITE IN A GRATITUDE JOURNAL

Each day, write down five things for which you are grateful. Be specific and vary what you write. Think back over the last twenty-four hours. What happened?

Did you see a beautiful flower? Write about it.

Did someone do something nice for you? Record it.

Are you grateful you kept your mouth shut and kept yourself out of trouble? Note it.

Did a friend help you with something? Write that in your journal.

After you write your five gratitudes, choose one and close your eyes. Spend sixty seconds immersed in the memory of that experience. This is not only a very relaxing exercise, it also strengthens your receptive powers.

## 4. SAY THANK YOU

Look for opportunities to thank people. Everywhere you go are people who make your days easier and more enjoyable and help the ones you love. Thank them! Send thank-you cards, letters, notes, or emails.

Thank the crossing guard who helps your child safely cross the street.

Thank your relatives for remembering your birthday.
Thank a friend for listening when you need to talk.
Thank your doctor for answering your questions.

## 5. GIVE

Who helps you? Who makes your life better? Express your gratitude by doing something or giving something to those who make a positive contribution to your life.

Pick flowers from your yard to give to a friend.
Offer to return books to the library for a busy neighbor.
Make a favorite meal for your spouse.
Give your child's teacher a gift card.

## { INSPIRING QUOTES }

*It is blessed to receive with grace and a grateful heart.*

° SARAH BAN BREATHNACH °

*Gratitude . . . turns problems into gifts, failures into success, the unexpected into perfect timing, and mistakes into important events.*

° MELODY BEATTIE °

*If we receive fully, gratitude follows naturally.*

∘ VICTORIA CASTLE ∘

*Appreciation can make a day, even change a life.*
*Your willingness to put it into words is*
*all that is necessary.*

∘ MARGARET COUSINS ∘

*We often take for granted the very things*
*that most deserve our gratitude.*

∘ CYNTHIA OZICK ∘

*Feeling grateful or appreciative of someone*
*or something in your life actually attracts*
*more of the things that you appreciate*
*and value into your life.*

∘ CHRISTIANE NORTHRUP ∘

*Gratitude helps you be receptive to*
*the life force of the universe.*

∘ DENISE LINN ∘

# Create Full Reciprocity in Your Relationships

Have you ever tried to change somebody? I have. It's exhausting. There is a reason that so many of us engage in this fool's errand. We have been taught that activity gets us what we want. If what we are doing is not working, the only thing we know to do is to try harder! Yet allocating 100 percent of our effort to trying to make something happen is mentally exhausting, physically depleting, and emotionally draining.

If you feel like you are giving more to a relationship than your partner is, stop and consider the following: The only possible match for someone who doesn't know how to receive is someone who doesn't know how to give.

Doesn't it make sense that if you are doing most of the giving and the doing, the compromising and accommodating, that the other person hangs back and doesn't feel that he or she needs to meet you halfway? It's human nature. But what you end up with is a project instead of a relationship.

You strengthen your receptive powers when you create the room for others to move toward you. This automatically shifts the balance of your relationships, not only with others, but also within yourself. And, as a result, people help you and give to you.

## Every Giver Has a Receiver and Every Doer Has a Taker

When you give and give and give to a person who does not thank you or acknowledge what you have given, your energy is drained rather than returned. This is why interacting with some people is so exhausting. They are like a well with a crack in it. They never feel filled up and want more and more and more. Receivers return energy to the giver by their appreciation for what has been given.

How can you get someone to be more giving when it seems like no matter what you say or do, they just take from you? You have probably already discovered that your kindness, compassion, or help does not encourage someone to give who doesn't want to give. The solution lies in breaking free from a doer-taker dynamic.

Our culture doesn't make a distinction between what you *do* and what you *give*. But there is a big difference between the two. When you *do*, you are operating out of a social role, like in these examples:

- A good friend loans money to her friends.
- A good wife cooks meals for her spouse.
- A good daughter calls her mother once a week.
- A good mother puts her child's needs before her own.
- A good employee works extra hours if she is needed.
- A good boss accommodates her employees' child care schedules.

These roles are based on social expectations of how you should behave irrespective of your feelings about them. It is not as if there is anything wrong with behaving in socially prescribed ways. But if you feel uncomfortable in a role and don't agree with it, not only do you feel the disconnection, other people feel it, too.

An example of this is the "stand by your man" philosophy that we saw over and over again when the wife of a misbehaving politician stood next to her philandering husband as he made a statement to the TV cameras.

It wasn't until people started to question the social necessity of this behavior that women began to opt out and let their husbands stand in the glare of the spotlight by themselves. This shift reflected the changing roles of women in our society as the public began to see the stand-by-your-man role as outdated and old-fashioned.

Consequently, instead of praising the suffering wife, we became uncomfortable with her deer-in-the-headlights gaze as she stood there and we collectively decided it was unnecessary. In 2009, when Jenny Sanford declined to join her husband, Governor Mark Sanford, as he spoke publicly about his extramarital affair, the stand-by-your-man role went into the dustbins of history.

Many roles have disappeared as women have gained rights. Although social-role flexibility has brought greater reciprocity to many relationships, in others women are still trying to figure out how to create relationships in which they receive as much as they give.

If you continue to give to a person because you think that's how "one *should* behave," even when that person does not give back to you, you will feel exhausted by your interactions and, in time, you will also feel resentful.

Additionally, when you do things for people that they are perfectly capable of doing for themselves, you are enabling them to continue their selfish behavior. Not only are you not doing them a favor in the long run, you will never achieve reciprocity with an individual who is as unable to give as you are unable to receive.

Givers and receivers are a natural team. So are doers and takers. Givers and receivers feel renewed, replenished, and energized by their interactions with each other. Doers and takers feel drained, exhausted, and resentful by their interactions with each other.

## Doers and Takers and Money

Why are women such easy marks when it comes to money? Small-claims courts are filled with women trying to get their money back from ex-friends and ex-boyfriends, most of whom swear that the money given or the cosigned loan was a gift and not a loan. Most women never enter the legal system. They give up trying to get their money back, consoling themselves with the excuse that they are kind people who wouldn't turn down a person in need.

What motivates a woman to "lend" money, often repeatedly, to the same person who has not paid her back?

- She is afraid of conflict.
- She wants to think of herself as a "good" friend or a "good" person.
- She is unable to say no because she doesn't have any practice saying no.

- She doesn't want to admit to herself that she is being used.

Have you heard the sayings "Don't throw good money after bad" and "Don't lend money you can't afford to lose"? So many people do not pay back money that the results from a google search show almost four million entries with information, warnings, axioms, and strategies for getting money returned from unwilling recipients. But a refusal to repay is not only an epidemic among people who know one another, it's also a problem in society and in governments.

The irony in these doer-taker relationships is that the people who receive the money are angry at the person who gave it to them for trying to get it repaid! Here is an example:

When Brenda's friend asked for money to pay bills, she didn't hesitate to get a cash advance on her credit card, even though she was financially struggling—in part because she was still paying back a bank loan, money she had borrowed for a now ex-boyfriend who refused to pay her back.

While she gave up on the ex-boyfriend, when her now ex-friend refused to pay her back, she decided to fight to get it. She was able to finagle this person, who was now angry and resentful, to make monthly payments—payments that she has to remind her each month to pay. She counts herself lucky that she is getting any money.

How you handle your money and think about your finances is an excellent barometer with which to assess all of your relationships. If you are a doer, there are plenty of people who will be happy to take your money, your time, and your energy. Here is another example where a financial transaction shows a lack of reciprocity—this time, between a company and a woman.

Lilly Ledbetter worked for the Goodyear Tire and Rubber Company for ten years. After she retired, she discovered that they had not paid her the same amount for the same work as her male counterparts. She filed a lawsuit and her case eventually ended up in the Supreme Court, which ruled against her. Why? Because she had not filed suit within 180 days of her first paycheck and therefore the statute of limitations had expired. Ms. Ledbetter did not know at that time that she was being paid less than the men. Congress rectified this injustice with the passage of the Lilly Ledbetter Fair Pay Act of 2009. Now, the 180-day statute of limitations begins each time a new paycheck is issued.

Are you impeding the natural flow of a give-receive relationship by not asking others to be fair? If you stop doing, others will stop taking. If you start receiving, you will open up a space as big as the Grand Canyon for others to give to you.

# The Journey, the Road, the Landscape, and the Traffic

Just as financial transactions provide insight into relationship dynamics, so do your driving habits. Which of the following examples most closely describe your relationships? Include not only your intimate partners, but also the other people in your life.

- Two-way street: Both people give and receive.
- One-way street: One person does most of the giving.
- Dead end: Has no future.
- Cul-de-sac: Has a limited future.
- Roundabout: You and your partner go around the same things again and again.
- Highway to heaven: A smooth ride for the most part with occasional off-ramps into the land of drama, but you and your partner are able to successfully get back on the highway.
- Country road: Slow, steady, and comfortable.
- Mountain road: Peaks and valleys, with high highs and low lows.

## While you are on the road, how do you and your partner-drivers behave?

- Do they wave to you to go first at the stop sign (considerate and patient)?

- Do they tailgate you (intimidation)?

- Do they make rude gestures or honk their horn (aggressive)?

- Do they yell at you (rage-aholic)?

- Do they follow you, corner you, and get out of their car (dangerous)?

- Do they purposely drive slower than the speed limit (passive-aggressive)?

- Do they speed (cause you to be hypervigilant in order to stay out of their way)?

- Do they text and drive (complete and total disregard for you)?

## Which of the following best resembles communication in your relationship?

- A green light: A good flow and moving energy; both people talk and listen.

- A red light: No or little conversation.

- A yellow light: Caution—you tiptoe around difficult conversations and resist bringing something up because you are afraid of conflict or because you feel that the other person will not respect your wishes, or you will have to fight to be heard, or you are afraid of the consequences.

- A blinking light: Go, stop, go, stop. Delay tactics and deflection. "Let's wait and see" or "I'll think about it and get back to you." That "getting back to you" never happens. This is a person who will commit to neither yes nor no.

- A broken light: Where do you stand in the relationship? Is the person present at all? Do you frequently break up and get back together? Are you involved in a secret relationship? Do you, in reality, even have a relationship?

## A Two-Way-Street Relationship

What is the best relationship you have today? This person may be an intimate partner, a friend, a child, a coworker, a boss, a parent. (Don't include your pet, no matter how adorable and wonderful!) Who is it with? What makes it so enjoyable? Be specific. What are the features of this relationship? Does your partner do any of the following?

- Lets you know how important you are to him or her.
- Listens to you and appreciates what you have to say.
- Enjoys your company.
- Respects your boundaries.
- Includes you in activities.
- Is fair and knows how to compromise.
- Thinks about your needs as much as hers or his.
- Doesn't view disagreement as threatening.
- Contributes to the relationship just as much as you do.

# One-Way, Dead-End, Cul-de-Sac, and Roundabout Relationships

If you are not getting back what you are putting into a relationship, you are likely to experience the following:

- You feel taken for granted.
- You feel like you are doing the lion's share of the work of the relationship.
- You don't feel heard.
- You don't feel your desires are respected.
- You feel you have to fight to get your point of view heard.
- You feel anxious.
- You feel stressed, exhausted, resentful, or overwhelmed.
- You feel emotionally drained.
- You feel afraid.

Your attitudes, behaviors, beliefs, and actions all say something about relationship reciprocity, or lack of it. Most relationships are neither all good nor all bad. Your honest assessment about the parts of your relationships you want and the parts you don't want gives you a starting point and a foundation on which you can build.

# The Cost of Caring

If you are continually giving more than 50 percent to a relationship, you are giving too much. If you are taking care of someone who is unable to give back due to an illness or another reason, however, you replenish your energy when you seek out support from those who are able to help you.

The majority of caregivers are women. We suffer the financial costs as well as emotional and physical health repercussions from providing long-term care for family members. Many of us receive little or no support, including from family members. The truth is that both people and our society count on women not bothering others for help. Because our culture is infatuated with people who do everything by themselves, you may find it difficult to step out of the caregiver role and into your humanity.

How do you take care of yourself when so much of your time is devoted to caring for others? How do you get reciprocity? How do you replenish emotionally, mentally, and physically?

- By asking for help
- By insisting that family members do their fair share
- By not giving up if you don't receive help the first time you ask

- By accepting help when it's offered
- By attending support groups or receiving counseling
- By spending social time with friends and loved ones

In the twenty-first century, women are still building a foundation for equality. If you are exhausted much of the time, you won't have the energy to do your part. Reciprocity requires your participation.

## Friendship Reciprocity

Ideally, your friends are the people who add to your life, are honest with you when you need them to be, lift you up when you are down, celebrate your successes, and listen when you need to talk.

Many years ago, I made friends with people I could help. Being needed by someone was, for me, the definition of a friendship. If I could do something for them, listen to their problems, and offer advice, I was content. Except I wasn't. I was in doer-taker relationships and didn't know it.

When I began to study the topic of receiving in the late eighties and early nineties, it finally occurred to me that my friends should be as interested in me as I was in them. To say that this was a revelation is an understatement. Prior to studying receiving, I just didn't get it.

When I began to speak up, include myself in my friendships, and stop being so darn helpful, some of the people I knew walked away. But a miracle occurred. As I shed my doer role as "helpful friend," I began to meet people who wanted to give to me as much as I wanted to give to them.

How do you see your role as a friend? Do you and your friends help one another? Does your life feel richer for knowing them? Television personality and philanthropist Oprah Winfrey and her best friend, Gayle King, have known each other for over three decades, and still have fun together and enrich each other's lives.

All women have benefited from the friendship between Elizabeth Cady Stanton and Susan B. Anthony, two determined women who never stopped advocating for women's rights, including the right to vote. If you are going to change history and advocate for your rights, a friend who "gets" you and will work as hard as you do to succeed in your goal makes life more rewarding, interesting, and meaningful.

## Match Me or Raise Me

Several years ago, when I moved from the East Coast to the Southwest, what I wanted more than anything else was to meet caring, kind people and create relationships that added to my life. I was exhausted by participating in dead-end relationships.

I created a motto, "Match Me or Raise Me," as a reminder to carefully consider relationship choices as I explored my new environment. I didn't want relationship projects anymore. I wanted reciprocity. I wanted relationships with people who were a good match for me. I also wanted to meet people who would raise me up, who would inspire me by who they were, what they were doing, and what they had accomplished.

I met plenty of people, some who were wonderful but who just weren't a good match for me, and so I moved on. I also met people who realized I was not a good match for them, and they moved on, too! This motto continues to help me to be a giver and not a doer, and has helped me open my heart to receive all of the goodness that is in people and in the world.

## 50/50

All of the tasks that you perform day in and day out can eat up every minute of your day. In the workplace and in education, women have been gaining equality by leaps and bounds. But at home, women still do the majority of household tasks.

The following are examples of household chores. How many do you do and how many do family members do?

- Wash dishes.
- Dry dishes.
- Load the dishwasher.
- Empty the dishwasher.
- Walk the dog.
- Feed the dog or other pets.
- Vacuum.
- Cut the lawn.
- Rake leaves.
- Set the table.
- Shop for groceries.
- Make the meals.
- Wash, dry, and fold the clothes.
- Put the clothes away.
- Pay the bills.
- Spend time playing with your children.
- Get your children ready for bed.
- Read a story to your children.
- Walk your children to the bus stop.
- Drive your children to school.
- Buy clothes for your children.

Create reciprocity in your family relationships by distributing the tasks of daily living so everyone is doing their fair share.

## Fear of Conflict

I believe fear of conflict is the single biggest obstacle that prevents women from creating reciprocity in their relationships. When we are unwilling to face conflict, we never get any experience or develop the skill needed to deal with people who are intent on not compromising.

Part of maturing is learning how to speak to those who do not agree with you without freaking out, crying, or raising your voice. If you never get any practice, you will never learn how to deal with unpleasant people or approach difficult topics and conversations.

When avoidance becomes a chronic way of relating, you undermine your relationships. You don't give people the opportunity to know you. This ongoing evasiveness becomes a destructive force in your relationships. No one is empowered by deflecting, hiding, and deceiving. Here are examples:

- Sandy loaned money to "friends" who did not pay her back and was unable to talk to them about returning her money.

- Mary is unable to tell her husband what will sexually satisfy her.

- Betsy is married to a man whom she lets make all of the decisions.

- Donna is so anxious about telling a friend that she won't be able to afford to rent his house that it keeps her up at night.

- Sarah breaks out in hives every time she thinks about telling her mother that she doesn't want to spend every Sunday dinner with her.

Receptive power is staying power. Even if you are uncomfortable with conflict and of hearing the word "no," start practicing reciprocity by speaking up. Don't give up. Women have a habit of giving up too soon. We cave. We don't stand our ground. We resist setting a boundary or limit. We don't use the word "no" enough. Unfortunately, what happens when you are uncomfortable saying no is that you form relationships with people who say it all the time.

## Bully in the House

Thank goodness, the topic of children being bullied in school has become a national conversation. It's distressing to see children intentionally inflict harm on other children. Where did they learn to do this?

Yes, children see violence on TV where they see people

treating others with little respect. But much of the role-modeling for this destructive behavior can be found closer to home—*in* their home. When women are bullied by their partners, the kids notice. How could they not?

## You may accept or condone unacceptable behavior from others for any of the following reasons:

- You want to keep the peace.
- You are afraid of conflict.
- You don't have the energy to deal with what will follow if you say something.
- You don't think it will do any good, since it hasn't previously.
- You don't want to admit to yourself that you are being treated poorly.
- You are afraid you will lose your relationship if you speak up.
- You are afraid of what will happen if you stand up for yourself.
- You are simply not in the practice of advocating for your own needs, so you don't know how to do it.

Read the following descriptions of
bullying from Wikipedia. See if you
recognize any of them.

- Bullying is the use of force or coercion to abuse or
  intimidate others.
- Bullying consists of three basic types of abuse:
  emotional, verbal, and physical.
- Bullying is characterized by an individual behaving
  in a certain way to gain power over another person.
  Direct bullying involves a great deal of physical
  aggression. Indirect bullying is characterized by
  attempting to socially isolate the victim.

I found it interesting that in a comprehensive section on
bullying, and one in which Wikipedia lists all of the areas
where bullying takes place and with whom, intimate relationships is not on the list. It's just not a word we use to
describe our mates. Instead we say:

- My partner is difficult.
- My partner refuses to listen to me.
- My partner won't compromise.
- My partner is in a bad mood.
- My partner is just having a bad day.
- My partner had a difficult upbringing.

Words have power, and I believe calling a bully a bully is a kind of liberation.

Mistreatment does not occur only in intimate relationships. Many women are treated poorly by their bosses, co-workers, friends, and family members—even by their own children. Do you experience any of the following?

- People who do not see your time as valuable as their time.
- People who talk about their day, problems, and joys but never ask you about yours.
- People who don't listen when you talk.
- People who ask you to do things for them but never offer to do things for you.
- People who physically abuse you.
- People who disregard your feelings, desires, and needs.
- People who criticize and demean you.

## A society or culture can also abuse as in the following examples:

- A society that does not pay women the same as men for equal work.
- A society that treats women as sexual objects.
- A society whose laws do not give women the same opportunities as they give men.

- A society that fails to educate men to not act violently against women or mete out harsh penalties for those who do.

- A society that does not teach women how to protect themselves from violence.

- A society that does not give equal rights and social benefits to lesbian, gay, bisexual, and transgender couples.

Healthy reciprocation occurs when both people in a relationship are not limited by law in what they have the right to do and choose. The individual who has rights has a cultural green light to discriminate against those who do not have rights.

In 1974, my mother had been separated from my father for one year when she found a house to buy. With a good job and having recently obtained her master's degree in social work, she was shocked to discover that, as a separated woman, she could not legally get a mortgage and would need to have her estranged husband cosign. My mother was fortunate that my father agreed to cosign. In the summer of 1974, the United States Congress passed the Depository Institutions Amendments Act, which gave women the legal right to obtain a loan.

# Strengthen Your Connections

Think of everybody as your partner in reciprocity. You have relationships with your mate, friends, children, parents, relatives, neighbors, bosses, employees, coworkers, colleagues, acquaintances, the people with whom you do business (store clerks, bank tellers, and vendors, to name a few), and even your government. You have plenty of people with whom you can practice strengthening your receptive powers. Don't settle for unequal relationships. You reclaim your half of the universe when you create full reciprocity in your relationships. Get started with the following exercises.

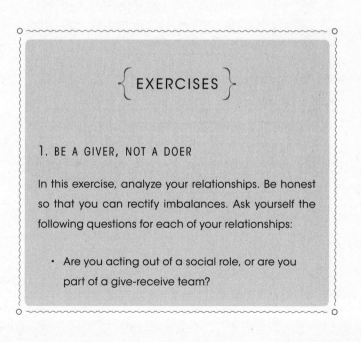

{ EXERCISES }

## 1. BE A GIVER, NOT A DOER

In this exercise, analyze your relationships. Be honest so that you can rectify imbalances. Ask yourself the following questions for each of your relationships:

- Are you acting out of a social role, or are you part of a give-receive team?

- Are you exhausted by your interactions, or are you strengthened by your connections?
- Do you and the other person each give 50 percent to the relationship?
- Are you enabling taker behavior?
- Are you ignoring bad behavior?
- Is the other person a taker or a receiver?
- Are you a giver or a doer?

## 2. STRENGTHEN YOUR RECEIVE MUSCLES

Spend time each day strengthening your receptive powers. Every time you immerse yourself in receptive states, you strengthen your receive muscles. You can do it in any of the following ways:

- Be present and notice what goes on in your environment.
- Listen to people when they talk to you.
- Pay attention to your feelings.
- Every day, think, say, and write down all of the things for which you are grateful.
- Accept compliments, gifts, and offers of help.

### 3. SPEAK UP AND DON'T GIVE UP

Give a voice to your ideas, desires, and preferences. Don't run away from difficult discussions. Communicate clearly and maturely. What is negotiable and nonnegotiable? Practice!

### 4. SHED SOCIAL ROLES

Be authentic and embrace your complexity. Examine your social roles and determine which behaviors feel authentic to you and which ones don't fit the person you are today. Think about it. Write about it.

### 5. CREATE TWO-WAY-STREET RELATIONSHIPS

Do the people with whom you spend time care as much about you as you do about them? How do they show their affection? Do you feel energized and happy to be in their presence? Or do you feel anxious? Make a list of the people you know. Are there any that, by cutting loose, you would gain energy? Which people would you like to spend more time with, and why?

## { INSPIRING QUOTES }

*Discover that you have two hands, one for helping*
*yourself and the other for helping others.*

◦ AUDREY HEPBURN ◦

*It's really important to receive love and compassion.*
*It is as important as being able to give it.*

◦ PEMA CHÖDRÖN ◦

*Being received by others into the most private*
*and intimate spaces of their lives . . .*
*is a moment of grace.*

◦ LOUISE PHIPPS SENFT ◦

*Love and kindness are never wasted. They bless*
*the one who receives them, and they bless the giver.*

◦ BARBARA DE ANGELIS ◦

*Get in the habit of receiving the benefits*
*of the things you do.*

◦ ELAINE ST. JAMES ◦

*When you truly give up trying to be whole
through others, you end up receiving
what you always wanted from others.*

∘ SHAKTI GAWAIN ∘

*To be fully seen by somebody, then, and be
loved anyhow—this is a human offering
that can border on miraculous.*

∘ ELIZABETH GILBERT ∘

# Don't Put Yourself Last or *You* Won't Last

D o you intentionally inflict stress on yourself? Filling your days with activities that your body cannot comfortably support is a kind of madness. But if you follow a cultural model that champions activity and self-sufficiency and undervalues receptivity and cooperation, you can't help but harm yourself. I call this "multitasking mayhem."

If you have been doing the exercises that I've given you in Steps One through Five, you have already experienced health benefits. Anybody who immerses in the pool of receptivity has experienced its healing powers.

For those of you who continue to regularly exceed your energy limits to give time and attention to others and invest in activities that leave you feeling

depleted and exhausted, it is my hope that after you finish reading this chapter, you will come to your senses. I mean that figuratively and literally.

You already know that eating healthy foods and exercising are good for you. I am not going to tell you what you already know. There are plenty of books, articles, and websites that give you information that helps your overall health. I include a list of excellent books on these topics in the Resources section.

In this chapter, I want to shed light on the backstory. I believe much of our stress and its health consequences can be traced to these:

- Avoiding conflict
- Giving up too soon

I've already addressed these topics in earlier chapters. Now I want to connect the dots among conflict avoidance, giving up too soon, and stress. I'll start with an example about boundaries.

## When Does "No" Mean "No"?

I received the following letter from a woman who asked me how to handle a situation when someone wants to give you something that you don't want to receive:

*Hi, Amanda,*

*People insist on giving me stuff I don't want, even if I try to be tactful and deter them (lots of books, products, etc., also from people who hope I'll promote their work).*

*And it often seems like a situation with friends where regifting (which I have noooo problem with, except it does feel a bit sleazy) is not an option. In those situations, the person is around, would look for their item, notice it was gone, and be hurt/insulted. And so I'm expected to be all grateful (I'm not) and actually use it. I really hate clutter in the first place and now live in a studio in a senior building where there just isn't room for stuff to pile up that I don't want or need. Very little shelf room for books——I got rid of hundreds of them. I'm at a stage of life where I find material goods a burden.*

*So this morning I was working in our community room library, my volunteer work here, and this charming old fellow in his late eighties I am fond of said he knew I was a book collector (I'm not) and he was going to give me a book for my collection (I don't have one).*

*He went upstairs and brought back a fairy-tale book, a nice one beautifully illustrated and probably worth a bit. I tried to deter him tactfully, saying it was too valuable and if we put it in the library it would probably get stolen (it would).*

*He said, no, no, it was just for me. Proud that he could give me something of value. Gahhh!!!! I couldn't refuse without hurting his feelings, and what if he ever wants it back. Any advice would be appreciated.*

*Donna*

I replied with the following:

*Dear Donna,*

*I love your question! This is really an issue about how and where we place our boundaries and what we do when people don't honor them. This predicament has so many applications.*

*As I discuss in* The Power of Receiving, *receiving is not a passive state. It's quite dynamic. Receiving our feelings, being willing to disappoint people, and being okay with feeling uncomfortable takes practice. Many of us were raised to tend to other people's feelings at the expense of our own. When you don't have enough practice receiving—in this case, receiving and honoring your own feelings—it is hard to hold your ground.*

*To illustrate this predicament, let's raise the stakes:*

*If someone wanted to take you out to dinner for a date and you didn't want to go, would you say "Thanks, but no," even if they insisted? If someone wanted to have sex with you and you didn't want to, would you say no even if that person badgered you?*

*How high do the stakes need to be to honor your feelings?*
*How willing are you to risk the other person's disappointment,*
*anger, sadness, discomfort, etc.? Here is a practice script with*
*the charming eighty-year-old:*

"*I know you are a collector of books.*"

"*I'm not!*"

"*But I want to give you a book of fairy tales!*"

"*Very sweet of you! But please give it to someone else. I have*
*no room in my apartment for anything!*"

"*I am going to go get it and give it to you.*"

"*I can't accept it. But thank you.*"

*The man returns with the book . . .*

"*I thank you for thinking of me, but I can't accept it. I am*
*not a book collector and I have no room in my apartment.*"

"*Take it!*"

"*No.*"

"*Take it!*"

"*No!*"

"*Take it, because it will make me happy!*"

"*Thank you, but no!*"

"*But you are the person I want to give it to! Take it!*"

"*Thank you, but no!*"

*There are plenty of people in the world who will not honor*
*your boundaries. You must honor them. It is not someone*
*else's job.*

*You can gracefully refuse to take the book while still*
*honoring his desire to give it to you. It may take a few*
*minutes, but then the exchange will be done. You won't have to*
*worry about him finding out what you do with the book. You*
*won't have to worry about what* you *will do with it. You will*
*not have to even think about it anymore.*

*The more practice you have receiving, the easier it is*
*to honor your feelings, your boundaries, and your limits.*
*Luckily, we live in a world where you will be able to get lots*
*of practice!*

*Amanda*

○ ○ ○

DO YOU SEE the stress that results from this single interaction? Now multiply it by hundreds and thousands of interactions with people who don't respect your boundaries, don't pay attention to what you say, and don't listen to you. Add to that the number of times that you never even spoke up to say no, which means that *you* did not respect your boundaries or listen to yourself.

Can you imagine a man spending the time, energy, and angst over this book of fairy tales? When men say no, people pay attention. When women say no, many people—men and women—trample right over that "no." Why? Because we are conflict avoiders.

Giving in because someone wants something for you that you do not want for yourself gives you relief in the short term. But it adds to your stress in the long run. And that stress begins to have a deleterious effect on your body. Here is a story about conflict avoidance and giving up too soon, both of which hampered my plans to leave a relationship:

After days of anguish, I finally decided that the best and right thing for me to do was to break up with my boyfriend. I knew in my heart that no matter how much I loved him, the relationship had no future for me, or at least not a good one. So, decision made. Whew! Onward!

That evening, I told him that I wanted to end the relationship and the reasons why. The next morning when we sat down to breakfast, it became increasingly clear to me that he had no idea that I had broken up with him! *Have I mastered the art of subtlety,* I wondered. *Or, is he so used to tuning me out that he didn't even hear me?*

With a sinking heart, I realized I was going to need to break up with him *again*. I was bleary-eyed and exhausted from breaking up with him the evening before and a sleepless night of thinking through the logistics of the breakup and the unknown aspects of my future. I just didn't have it in me to do it all over again.

I waited weeks before initiating another conversation about breaking up. This time, I made sure I was crystal clear and made sure that he understood what I was saying.

### Here are some situations when you may have said something but people paid no attention:

- Asking your children to clean their bedrooms
- Telling your kid to turn off the computer, turn out the lights, and go to sleep
- Asking your spouse to help with housework
- Asking your boss for relief from too much work
- Asking your friend to pay back the money she owes you
- Asking a family member to walk the dog
- Asking your spouse to pick up groceries on the way home from work
- Asking a neighbor to keep the music down in the evening
- Asking a family member to turn the television sound down
- Asking a coworker to not talk to you when you are trying to get your work done

When people don't listen to you, what do you do? Do you give up and do it yourself? Do you think that it just isn't worth it to keep bringing up the same thing over and over? Do you feel angry or resentful? Does your stress level go up? Do you do any of the following?

- Ruminate
- Overthink
- Worry
- Complain
- Obsess
- Cry

## Here are some of the results of conflict avoidance and of giving up:

- Not parenting your children. (I don't have enough energy.)
- Staying in a destructive relationship. (I don't want to be alone.)
- Working in a job you hate. (The economy prevents me from looking elsewhere.)
- Pretending that you are healthy. (I need to lose only a few pounds.)

## What kind of coping mechanisms do you employ?

- Eat too much.
- Eat too little.

- Drink.
- Shop.
- Sleep.

A symptom of conflict avoidance and giving up too soon is found in the following examples:

- I can't make myself exercise.
- I can't make myself get enough sleep.
- I can't make myself eat healthy foods.
- I can't make myself say no to my children.
- I can't make myself disappoint people.
- I can't make myself ask for what I want.

Pharmaceutical companies prey on us, eager to make, market, and sell us drugs. Do you take drugs for any of the following reasons?

- To sleep
- To stay awake
- To cope
- To feel less anxious
- To feel less depressed
- To concentrate

## Renew ~ Replenish ~ Refuel

Does being tired feel normal? Is your immune system fragile?

The Center for Disease Control and Prevention reports that autoimmune diseases affect approximately 8 percent of the population, 78 percent of whom are women. Now that's a statistic to give one pause.

Some years ago, I belonged to a book club. Most of the women were in their forties. One day, before the book discussion began, one of the women mentioned that she took a medication for a hypothyroid (an autoimmune disease). The eight other women said they were on the same medication. I asked them what the symptoms were that had led their doctors to prescribe the medication. They had told their doctors that they were tired most of the time. What surprised me was that none of these women had considered that their fatigue may have been caused by their lifestyle rather than a medical condition, especially since they all shared the same symptom.

I don't know any of the details that resulted in these women being diagnosed with an autoimmune disease. But I do know that if you don't include many (if any) receptivities in your day, it makes sense that you would be tired. If you never replenish your energy, exhaustion is a logical result.

Everybody encounters times in life that are stressful. If

you already know how to relax and regularly engage in as many receptivities as activities throughout the day, when difficult times come you will benefit. Here is an example:

Dawn lost her job and was trying to sell her house and move to the Southwest. I asked her to list the top five things she does every single week. Here they are:

1. Clean (the house, laundry, dishes)

2. Cook meals

3. Walk in the park, with or without the dog

4. Do yoga

5. Socialize

I was surprised by her answers. I knew she was looking for work, I knew her house had been on the market for months, and I knew that she was eager to relocate. All three of these are known to be major stressors and there is no question that Dawn was feeling the stress of it all.

When I asked her about her job search, she told me that her job search had brought her into contact with people and groups she otherwise would never have known. She told me how inspired she felt by these people and that her social connections kept her spirits up during this difficult time.

What I know about Dawn is this: Prior to the stressors of a lost job, house sale, and relocation plans, she practiced yoga, kept in contact with people, and regularly went to the park, which is near her home but far enough away that she needs to drive to get there.

Out of her top five, she listed three receptivities and two activities. Three to two is a wonderful ratio. I believe she was able to keep this balance in spite of her difficulties because she had already cultivated a life where she valued time spent in receptivities just as much as she enjoyed her activities.

## Delegate

You already know there is so much more to you than being everyone's helper. Even Cinderella learned this lesson, and look at what she received—a fairy godmother, a great dress, and a handsome prince! The truth is, if you do not see your time and health as valuable, no one else will either. That won't change until you ask people to do their share. Here are a few examples of balancing your giving with receiving:

| Give | Receive |
| --- | --- |
| You cook the meal. | Your kids set the table. |
| You let your sister borrow your car. | She puts gas in the car. |
| You grocery shop. | Your child puts the groceries away. |

| | |
|---|---|
| You wash the dishes. | Your spouse takes out the garbage. |
| You drive your kids to school. | They put their backpacks, homework, etc., in the car. |
| You buy dog food. | Your daughter walks the dog. |

## Forced to Receive

Many people learn how to receive due to an illness or other situation that causes them to depend on others. Here is an example:

Melissa, a high-powered executive, had broken her foot. Crutches, and later a walker, made it difficult to get around. She told me her husband was able to help her. I asked her if this experience had changed the way she thought about receiving help in general.

She proceeded to answer a question I had not asked. A few minutes later, I asked her again. Just like the first time I asked, it was as if she had not heard the question as she answered something I had not asked. Much later in the conversation, I asked her again and she told me that she found it very frustrating to ask her husband to do things that she could not do, although she made a point of saying that he was very willing to do so. She also told me that she had gotten tired of asking.

"Did you have to ask every single time?" I asked her. "Yes," she told me. She had solved her dilemma by hanging a bag on her walker and hobbling around the house. She told me that she wanted things done a certain way and that it was easier to do it herself than to ask. I hear that last statement from women a lot. Is this about fear of conflict? Is this about control or preference? What is the difference between control and preference?

When you control, you say, "It's my way or the highway." You are being unreasonable. That's not a two-way-street relationship. When you have a preference, you are letting people know what you want. You make a request. When the person does not do what you have asked, you have three solutions:

- Ask every single time.
- Have the conversation that needs to be had so that you don't have to ask for the same thing repeatedly.
- Just do it yourself.

If we could have only the conversations where we could predict a positive outcome, we would never have any conversations at all! So, what if people don't cooperate? You have an opportunity to practice facing conflict.

We try to control people when we don't trust them. There may be very good reasons for not trusting some people. Do you really think that people keep "forgetting" to do what they said they would do? Could it be that they know if they don't do it or don't do it properly, that you will do it and they will be off the hook?

Let's review.

Here are examples of a person who can ask only for what she wants when the following conditions are met:

- What you want doesn't make others uncomfortable, upset, or angry.
- What you want doesn't interfere with what people want for themselves.
- What you want doesn't interfere with what someone else wants for you.
- Others approve of what you want.

Here are examples of a person who speaks up and exercises her receptive power:

- You remain calm when another person is riled up or uncooperative.
- You listen to what someone has to say even if you disagree.
- You insist that others not speak disrespectfully and you are willing to walk away if they disregard your request.

- You refuse to do something that goes against your values, morals, or beliefs.

- You advocate for your own needs.

- You withhold something that the other person wants until they meet you halfway.

- You stand up for yourself.

- You don't give up.

I know many women who will ask but when the answer is no, or if the other person doesn't cooperate, they cave immediately and move on. Women are very used to moving on and taking care of the things that people said they would do, but don't.

"It's not worth the aggravation," you may say.

"I have better things to do with my time than checking up on (fill in the blank)."

"If anything is going to get done right, I will have to do it."

Can you see how this approach prolongs untenable situations, contributes to stress, causes you to reach for unhealthy substances to dampen your feelings, and ultimately leads to poor health?

In the next section, I show you how to move through your day in a way that fills you up, brings you peace, and gives you courage to face some of the harder conversations with yourself and with others.

## Come to Your Senses

How many times have you rushed through your day ignoring the sights, sounds, smells, tastes, and textures that surround you? With so much going on these days, pausing to reflect, assess, and receive may seem impossible. From the weather to the economy to stressful personal or family situations, we can forget to just take a moment and breathe.

It's so easy to get caught up in the events of our lives and ride them like a runaway train. But just as I've talked about your relationship to conflict, to money, to drivers, and to people, you also have a relationship with your body.

If you are inconsiderate of your body's needs and desires, it won't like it. Nobody and no thing wants to be treated disrespectfully or shoddily. Your body is not meant to be a workhorse or a repository for the things you don't want to face.

If you view ongoing stress as natural, you will try to manage it or compensate for it. I don't want you to manage it. I want you to eliminate it. One way to do that is to see, hear, touch, taste, and smell your environment by engaging the millions of receptors that are a part of your five senses.

When you are sense-absorbed, your busy mind retreats and your worries are a million miles away. Think about it. Isn't it true that your mind is calm when, for example, you watch a beautiful sunset, smell baking bread, or listen to birds singing?

In the following section, I show you how to enter a receptive state through your five senses. Tune in to them every day and you will automatically become more relaxed, less stressed, happier, and healthier. The more relaxed you are, the stronger you become and the more you will be able to confront conflict, be true to yourself, and do what you know in your heart is good for you.

## The Scents to Smell

When we use the phrase "stop and smell the roses," we are saying, "Slow down and enjoy life." There is a biological basis for this axiom. When you smell something, what has occurred is that the molecules that carry the smell have contacted your olfactory receptors. These receptors are located in an area close to the part of the brain that regulates emotion. The sense of smell is the sense most closely associated with our emotions.

Which scents make you feel relaxed, happy, content, or secure? It's not the same for everybody, so find the right ones for you. Experiment. Introduce your receptors to new smells. If something doesn't smell good, do something about it! Be considerate. Don't subject your receptors to something they don't like.

Research has shown that noticing and appreciating (both are receptive states) a scent increases your ability to smell it. So, when you love a smell, pay extra attention in order to multiply its effects. Here are examples:

- The aroma of baking bread
- The perfume of flowers
- The smell of wood burning in a fireplace
- The scent of the ocean
- The fragrance of spices and herbs
- Freshly cut grass

When you take deep, full breaths, you not only engage your olfactory receptors, you also stimulate the parasympathetic nervous system, which helps you relax. If you are upset and angry, what do people tell you to do? Take ten deep breaths. What they are saying is, "Calm down." The next time you feel distressed, find something lovely to smell and breathe deeply. From that relaxed, receptive state, you will find a solution to what is bothering you.

## A Feast for the Eyes

The receptors that are responsible for detecting light and allowing us to see are called "photoreceptor cells." These cells send signals to your brain.

Choose what images and sights you want to show your receptors. During the day, spend time looking at things that bring you pleasure, that make you feel good, that are beautiful. Do it purposefully. Think of it as doing something nice for your receptors so that they don't have to see the same things day in and day out. Give them something pretty to look at. Give your receptors variety. Look at things that are far away and things that are up close. Before you go to bed at night, don't watch disturbing or stimulating images on television. Instead, look at something calming.

Sleep experts tell us not to watch television or stare at computers or other light-emitting screens before we go to bed, because doing so inhibits the release of melatonin, a hormone that regulates sleep.

Can certain colors help you relax? Research suggests that colors such as red and yellow have a stimulating effect, while others such as blue and green have a calming effect. Be aware of the colors in your environment. Admire the green colors plentiful in nature and let your eyes drink in the soothing blue of the ocean or a pond.

Pay extra attention when you see something you like, in order to multiply its effects. Don't glance—admire. Here are examples:

- A sunset
- Birds flying

- Clouds drifting across a blue sky
- Art
- Flowers
- Children playing
- Dogs catching Frisbees

If you spend a lot of time in a visually unattractive environment, place a picture of a nature scene near you, choose a screen saver with beautiful images, or download an app that has gorgeous photographs. Look at the sky through a window or go outside. Every day, give your photoreceptors something to enjoy. Be creative. Look for beauty and you will find it.

## Sound Effects

Auditory receptor cells, called "hair cells," are responsible for turning sounds into electrical signals that are carried to the brain by sensory nerves.

Some sounds trigger stress and others relax you. Figure out which sounds soothe you and treat your nervous system to this enjoyable experience. Research has shown that dopamine, a neurotransmitter, is released when you listen to music that you like. Release stress by listening to pleasing sounds including these:

- Music
- Chants
- The sound of *om*
- The sound of water: rain, rivers, the ocean
- A person's voice

Soothe your nervous system by sitting quietly and listening to all of the sounds that you couldn't hear when your mind was busy thinking about all of the things you are busy doing. Here are some of the sounds you may hear if you are really quiet:

- The hum of the refrigerator
- The sound of children playing outside
- The wind rustling the leaves of a tree
- The creaks of a building
- The sound of traffic
- The ticking of a clock

Every time you engage your auditory receptors, you immerse yourself in a receptive state. The next time you are standing in line at a store, waiting for the bus, or sitting in your car at a red light, don't distract yourself. Open your ears and listen.

## Keep in Touch

Your skin contains millions of sensory receptors. Through them, you feel pain, heat, cold, and pressure. When you touch something you like, the stress hormone cortisol is lowered and the feel-good hormone oxytocin is released. Research has shown that premature babies gain more weight when they are held and that immune systems are strengthened by touch.

### Do you pay attention to what you touch or what touches you? Here are examples:

- A massage
- A shampoo and haircut
- The warmth of the sun on your skin
- A hug
- A supportive arm around your shoulder
- Holding hands
- Getting your back scratched
- A cool breeze
- Touching the fabric of your clothes
- Running your hands through water
- Planting flowers
- The feel of the sheets when you get into bed

- The scratch of a washcloth
- Brushing your hair

As you move through your day, be aware of what you touch and what touches you. Immerse yourself in that sensation. Multiply the benefits by paying attention. Don't chat while you are getting a massage. Notice how the wind feels on your face. Show your affection by hugging, touching someone's shoulder, or patting them on the back.

## Good Taste

Taste receptors, called "gustatory receptors," are cells located in the taste buds. They detect sweet, salty, sour, bitter, and savory tastes. Other receptors are involved when you taste: olfactory receptors for smell and a variety of sensory receptors to detect touch: hot, cold, pressure, and texture.

Do you pay attention to the taste of the food you eat every day? Do you eat the same food most of the time? Pay attention to your food. Does it lack flavor? Is it too salty or too sweet? Give your receptors variety by experimenting with different foods. Different receptors detect different tastes. For instance, don't overload the ones that detect sweetness and underuse the ones that detect savory flavors.

Try out different spices and different kinds of cuisine. When possible, choose organic products and food from local farmers markets. Or grow your own food. Relax and enjoy your food in the following ways:

- When you eat, create an enjoyable environment.
- Use pretty plates.
- Don't eat quickly.
- Sit down when you eat.
- Say a blessing.
- Thank your food.

In short, noticing is one of the most powerful of the receptive states. If we all simply noticed what is in our external and internal environments, I am convinced that our world would be more peaceful and we would be more relaxed and content.

Today, remind yourself to engage your senses. You can do it when you are in the car waiting for the light to turn green, when you are on hold on the phone, or when you are walking your dog. The beauty and miracle of receiving is that you can do it anytime and everywhere.

## Stress Is a Choice

The desires, needs, and activities of children, family members, and mates can and, for many women, do take an enormous amount of energy and time. But, if you do not accept stress as a natural part of your life, you will ask for the help that makes your life easier. To do that, you have to risk conflict. You have to stand your ground and not give up when people do not want to help you.

When you ask for what you need and receive what people and the world have to give, you open up pathways you couldn't see before, stimulate your imagination in ways that could not happen before, and have energy that was not previously available to you. Once you get used to a balanced, stress-free life, you will not consider sacrificing your health and emotional well-being. You will not put yourself last on your list. Why? This is what you would think:

- I want to get a good night's sleep so I will be alert during work tomorrow.

- I want to make sure I get enough protein today so I will have energy.

- I want to go to my yoga class so I will feel relaxed and centered.

- I want to leave work on time so I can enjoy time with my children.

Make a commitment today to bring more balance into your life—to receive as much as you give. Here are a few ideas to get you started:

- Ask family members to do their share: put breakfast dishes in the dishwasher or sink, walk the dog, or take books back to the library.

- Create a place where you can be alone, even if it is your bedroom with a *Do Not Disturb* sign on the door.

- Cultivate a social life. Get together with a friend. Go to the movies or meet for a meal.

- Practice and become comfortable with saying the word "no."

- Invest in your spiritual life, whether you read inspiring books, go to church, or spend time in nature's cathedral.

- Accept, with gratitude, compliments, gifts, and offers of help.

If you include *you* as an integral and important part of your vision for your relationships, family, and the world, not only will you become healthier and more energized, but your giving will no longer drain you—it will strengthen you.

{ EXERCISES }

## 1. PRACTICE FACING CONFLICT

When avoiding conflict is a default way to deal with people, you never get to the point when you can stand your ground or learn how to negotiate. Is there something that you need to say or do? Make a point this week to speak up or do what you need to do. I promise it will get easier over time.

## 2. BALANCE ACTIVITIES WITH RECEPTIVITIES

Aim for an equal balance each day between activities and receptivities. Put a list of receptivities where you can see them every day, and check them off after you have done them. If you realize you need to get in more receptivities before the end of the day, delegate something that is on your activity to-do list or save it for tomorrow and go out for a walk and treat your sense receptors to something pretty and enjoyable. Go to bed each night knowing that your activities and receptivities are balanced.

### 3. PRACTICE SAYING NO

Set clear boundaries and hold to them. Don't be so available. Don't be so flexible. Practice saying no without excusing, explaining, or equivocating. When you are not sure if you want to say yes or no, say "I'll think about it." Give yourself the time you need until you do know.

### 4. DON'T GIVE UP

Once you know what you need, don't lose heart, don't let people talk you out of it, don't cave. You know what's fair. You know you are not asking for something that isn't the right thing for people to do. Learn by observing people who are good at asking for what they want. What happens when they don't back down? Where do they get support? What makes them strong? Educate yourself.

### 5. COME TO YOUR SENSES

Choose one of your five senses and enjoy everything you receive through that sense for sixty seconds. You can do this exercise numerous times during the day and anywhere. You can do it when you are waiting for someone, when you are in line at the grocery store, when you eat a meal, when you go for a walk. Think of this exercise as exercising your receptors and treating them to something enjoyable. Be creative. Have fun with this exercise.

{ INSPIRING QUOTES }

*When you know it's time for action, act.*
*When you feel it's time to rest, rest. Not resting*
*is as harmful as not acting.*

∘ MARTHA BECK ∘

*When you start using senses you've neglected, your*
*reward is to see the world with completely fresh eyes.*

∘ BARBARA SHER ∘

*When one is pretending, the entire body revolts.*

∘ ANAÏS NIN ∘

*Certain activities, attitudes, foods, and persons*
*support the cultivation of an unconscious life.*
*They draw us away from our center. They throw*
*us off-balance. They deplete the soul.*

∘ PATRICIA LYNN REILLY ∘

*You must have authorship of your own destiny.*
*The pen that writes your life story must be held*
*in your own hand.*

∘ IRENE C. KASSORLA ∘

*Life is full of beauty. Notice it. Notice the bumble bee,*
*the small child, and the smiling faces.*
*Smell the rain and feel the wind.*

∘ ASHLEY SMITH ∘

*Pay attention.*
*Be astonished.*
*Tell about it.*

∘ MARY OLIVER ∘

# Be Respectful of Your Past, Have a Vision for Your Future, but Live in the Moment

We've come a long way together through the chapters and steps. By now, you know that receptivity is not an abstract concept. Receiving adds to your life in tangible ways. It gives you breathing room, space to relax, and new ideas and experiences.

When you are in a receptive state or engaged in a receptivity, you are automatically in the present moment. Your mind is not running through a to-do list for your future or picking through the events and people from your past. Even so, the burdens and joys that have come and gone are with you in each moment, just as your hopes for the future reside alongside your past. It's like you have taken a brush and dipped it into a myriad of colors and experiences, of hopes and dreams, and are painting a canvas that shows where you are right here, right now.

I began this book by acquainting you with all of the ways that receptivity influences your life. I encouraged you to claim the 50 percent, the receptive power that is your birthright. I talked about how important it is for us, as a group, to mature and behave in ways that we are proud of and that shines a positive light on our gender. I've asked us to do a better job at protecting girls from nefarious influences. I've asked you to quit focusing on your self-esteem, which I believe is a manufactured distraction designed by those who have a vested interest in degrading women for profit and control.

We are entering a new era, one in which women are coming out of the shadows and are participating in the world in ways that have not previously been possible. I believe that the more we embrace our receptive power, the more humanity will benefit.

The saying "A butterfly flapping its wings in South America creates a typhoon in Japan" is a potent way to think about the effect of personal actions and social movements. When you enter into your natural state where activity and receptivity are a team, the effects are huge, noticeable, and life-changing—not just for you, for everyone. You shift the energy and the conversation in your relationships, your community, your country, and the world.

The beauty and miracle of receiving is how easy it is to do, how effortless it is to enter into receptive states, how simple it is to integrate receptivities into your days, and how good it feels to fall into your natural state.

Are you ready to change your life? Are you willing to receive as much as you give by committing to the following?

- Experiencing conflict
- Standing your ground
- Getting to know your feelings
- Asking for what you want
- Seeking support
- Being grateful
- Advocating for your needs in a relationship
- Coming to your senses and integrating receptivities into your day

When you practice receptivity, you respect your past, but you don't live there. You have a vision for your future, but you don't live there either. Instead, you enter into the present moment, the fertile space that births everything you create.

## Respect the Past

My mother doesn't like to waste anything, whether the food on her plate or a piece of string on a package. Her mother was a young woman who raised two children during the Depression. I came into the world during a prosperous time when America was on the upswing and it looked like anything was possible. These days, my nieces and nephew are coming of age at a time when people need to conserve, resources are in jeopardy, and jobs are scarce. It seems humanity has come full circle.

We are all shaped by the times we are born into. For my grandmother, the Depression was a period of time that she had to endure, and she had to figure out the practical logistics of how to raise a family during a time of scarcity. My mother, born in 1929, was raised in a world where people struggled to make ends meet. For me, the Depression was something I read about in history books. Not until I was older did I understand the historical context for the choices I am free to make today.

To what extent did my grandmother and mother pay attention to their feelings, know what they wanted, or ask for help? Were they grateful for what they had? Did they even think about what a reciprocal relationship would look like? Did they suffer the consequences that come from putting themselves last?

# What Would Alice, Elizabeth, and Susan Think?

That's what I sometimes wonder, when I think about Alice Paul, Elizabeth Cady Stanton, Susan B. Anthony, and all of the other women who worked so hard to give us the rights we have today.

In the photographs I've seen of Susan B. Anthony, she looks like a stern version of my grandmother, and a bit intimidating. Actually, she was a determined, brilliant, and passionate woman who knew how to read and write when she was three years old. By the time she was seventeen years old, she was collecting petitions to abolish slavery.

Susan met Elizabeth Cady Stanton in Seneca Falls when she was thirty-one years old, and the two became fast friends. Together they founded the National Woman Suffrage Association and traveled throughout the United States giving speeches asking the government to grant women the same rights as men.

Susan was fifty-two years old when she was arrested, tried, and convicted for voting in the 1872 presidential election. After a contentious trial, she was fined a hundred dollars. She told the judge that she would not pay it, and she never did. Susan died in 1906, fourteen years before women were given the vote with the passage of the Nineteenth Amendment to the U.S. Constitution in 1920.

How do you show your respect for Alice, Elizabeth, Susan, and all of those women who dedicated their lives to making yours better? How do you express your gratitude? Do you treat your relationship to them as a one-way street and take what they did for granted? Do you honor them? How do you do that? Here are a few ideas:

- By taking advantage of the rights you have
- By helping to further and strengthen women's rights
- By paying it forward and helping women who live in countries without rights
- By voting
- By being informed about legislation that affects women
- By refusing to buy products that depict women in disrespectful ways
- By teaching your daughters and sons to treat women with respect
- By insisting that you be treated with respect
- By mentoring a young woman

To respect the past, you have to know your past. When did your country give women the right to vote? How many female elected representatives are in your country's governing bodies? While over forty countries have already had a female president or prime minister, I am still waiting for a woman to be elected president in my country, the United States. I know I will see it in my lifetime.

## What about You?

### You have a past, a personal history.

- How does your past contribute to the decisions you make today?

- What have you learned?

- What do you do differently today because of past experiences?

- What feelings do you have about people, events, or circumstances from your past?

- What do you feel grateful for that occurred in your past?

- What did you want and did you get it?

- Did you ask for help when you needed it?

- What were your relationships like?

- Did you put yourself last, or did you include your desires, needs, and preferences?

Respect your personal, family, and collective past. Receive it for whatever is there. You can like it, love it, hate it, or feel ambivalent about it. But don't run away, don't ignore it, don't hide from it, don't judge it, and don't live there. Just receive it.

# Have a Vision for Your Future

Your future arrives whether or not you have a vision for it. You may not notice it or appreciate it because you are busy talking on the phone, texting your friends, checking your Facebook status, cleaning your house, grocery shopping, or helping your kids with their homework, among your numerous activities.

The following story is about a woman who figured out what she wanted and created a beautiful vision for her future once she learned how to receive:

Judi had been a successful artist, and she and her husband had owned an art gallery. They lost their business and their house when the economic downturn occurred. They invested in a new business that had the potential to bring in a good income and, after a few years, they reached a modicum of financial stability. Judi spent her days doing tasks for the business, babysitting her grandchild, and doing all of the numerous chores that were part of her daily life. But she missed drawing and painting.

When Judi signed up for my Receive and Manifest classes, a five-week course that teaches people how to receive, she wanted to feel motivated to paint again but she didn't really know what she wanted to paint. Like a lot of women, she had only a vague idea about what she wanted. She was intrigued that she could find out what she wanted—not by pursuing activities, but by learning how to receive.

In the course, I began by asking the participants to write down what they wanted, using only one sentence. Judi decided to write: *I want to fill four pages in my sketchbook each week.* That was her first step. Throughout the five weeks, Judi applied each of the lessons as she dedicated herself to learning how to receive. She made rapid progress. By the time the course had ended, her goal was clear—she wanted to sell her work again and try her hand at a new genre, creating art for children. And that is exactly what she is doing now. She is painting and selling her artwork.

## Begin

A vision for your future has to start somewhere. Don't wait until you have a fully thought-out idea. Don't hesitate because you don't know what you want. Your goal will become clear once you begin. Think of it this way: Somebody has to start the conversation. When you write down your goal, that's what you do—you say the first words. Keep in mind that your goal will change over time. You will tweak it and change it more than once. You may even erase it and start from scratch with a new one.

What does your future hold? Start here: Write down

what you want. Create a vision board so that you have visual images to look at. Have conversations. Tell people what you are thinking about for your future. Ask them about theirs. Strengthen your receive muscles by receiving something every single day.

## Apply the lessons you've learned to support your plans for the future:

- What are your feelings about what you want?
- What does your intuition tell you?
- Do you know what you want, or do you need to find out?
- What help will you need to get there?
- What are you grateful for that is contributing to your plans for the future?
- Cultivate relationships with those who are as interested in your future as you are in theirs.
- Create the time and energy you need to fulfill your plans for the future.

## Who are the beneficiaries besides you when you invest in your future?

- Your family members benefit by seeing a woman respect herself enough that she is willing to invest in her future.

- Children see a woman who is courageous and determined, rather than a woman who talks about her self-esteem problems, her weight, her sacrifices, and her difficulties. That's a nice gift to pass on to the next generations.

- Society benefits by having half of the population contribute with enthusiasm and dedication.

- Women everywhere benefit by seeing you care enough about yourself that you are willing to step up—and out. We all could use more role models.

The past and the future are a team. One doesn't exist without the other. They are a way to measure time and experience and are useful for that. It is the place where both past and future are malleable. It is where both are interpreted. But, the present—that's where the power is.

## Live in the Moment

How do you live in the moment at the same time that you are respecting your past and having a vision for your future? What is this "being in the now" we hear so much about? Why is it a useful or good place to be? Keep reading.

It's relaxing to be present, which simply means that you are absorbed in what you are doing in that moment. It's not more complicated than that.

- You don't have competing agendas.

- You are not stressing about something that has already happened or may happen in the future.

- You are not making plans or going over a to-do list.

- You are not thinking about events and people from your past.

The present is a place that crowds out the past and the future. There's no room for them there. The moment is full enough without them.

When you are engaged in a receptivity, you are in that experience in that moment. Think about it. Isn't it true that when you, for example, taste a delicious food, or watch a beautiful sunset, or get a massage, you are enjoying that experience so fully that you don't really pay attention to anything else? Try to interrupt someone who is listening to their favorite song. They'll shush you.

Receptivity is your domain. Reclaiming your half of the universe requires you to spend time in receptive states. You cannot claim something you don't notice or don't know about. The information you receive from being in receptive states informs you about what you want, who it is you want to be with, where you want to go, and what you want to do.

## You Are Here

Years ago, my twin sister and I were at the local mall, standing in front of the map that shows the location of all of the stores. A yellow arrow pointed to a spot on the map with the words "You are here." My sister and I have a terrible sense of direction. If we were birds, we would fly north in the winter.

As we concentrated on the map, trying to figure out where we were in relation to all of the stores, my sister asked me, "How do they know we are here?" I laughed. Although I didn't know where we were in relation to anything else, I did know why the map knew where we were. "I'll tell you later," I said as we headed optimistically in the wrong direction.

## Where Are You?

Here you are at this moment in time, reading this book, at this age, in this part of your life-journey. Look around. What do you see, hear, and smell? Who is regularly in your environment—at home, at work, at school, in your community? These are your fellow travelers. Do you like them? Love them? How do they feel about you? What are you thinking, feeling, intuiting, wanting, accepting, creating, asking, or advocating for today?

Are you so busy barreling through your days that you have neither time nor energy to fully engage in what you are doing? Are you in the past, thinking about what you've done or a conversation you had? Or, are you in your future, thinking about the tasks ahead of you?

## The Big Circle

I created the Big Circle as a visual representation of the present. This is where you relax and recharge. Every time you enter a receptive state, you are in the Big Circle. When you do a receptivity, you are in the Big Circle. It's like a big battery. It's the place you plug into when you need energy coming in instead of energy going out. The more you have in your Big Circle, the more energized and fulfilled you are.

In the opening chapter to this book, I talked about how so much of the literature about reducing stress tells you to decrease your activities. I introduced you to the concept of adding receptivities. It's easier to think about what to add rather than what to subtract.

The diagram of the Big Circle is filled with receptivities. Create your own Big Circle and fill it up. Crowd out your worries, stresses, and problems. The things that bother you and the problems that seem unsolvable will resolve and become clear by spending time in your Big Circle.

# The Big Circle

Welcome

Listen    Accept

Daydream

Soak in a bathtub

Enjoy a cup of tea                    Allow

Knit

Pet your cat

Appreciate

Meditate        Taste        Draw

Read a book

Sleep

Look at the stars    Unwind

Notice

Paint            Reveal

Sit in the sun                Watch whales

Admire flowers

Acknowledge

Relax

Let go    Breathe        Pet your dog    Watch a sunset

Putter

Yield

Open

Feel    Nap

Garden

Attract                            Sit quietly

Watch clouds        Watch

Hug

Contemplate                        Embrace

Let it be        Slow down

Be

Taste chocolate    Feed the ducks

Go for a walk

Include

Spend time in nature

Get a massage                Rest

Do yoga

Count sheep

Sculpt

# { The Past, Future, and Present of Each Step }

Take a moment to reflect upon the past, future, and present for each of the preceding six steps. What have you learned? What choices will you make? What will you receive today?

## STEP ONE: Pay Attention to Your Feelings and Trust Your Intuition

The Past: What have you learned?
You use poor judgment when you don't include your feelings when you make decisions.

The Future: What's next?
Listen to what your intuition tells you.

Today: What will you receive?
Receive your feelings about the people in your life, the work you do, the friends you have.

## STEP TWO: Know What You Want

The Past: What have you learned?
Your desires are as important as everyone else's.

The Future: What's next?
Each day, write down five things for which you are grateful.

Today: What will you receive?
Receive everything. Decide later.

## STEP THREE: Ask for Help If You Need It and Accept It When It's Offered

The Past: What have you learned?
Don't turn away what people want to give because of old-fashioned ideas about pride.

The Future: What's next?
Seek support to help you accomplish your goals.

Today: What will you receive?
Receive compliments, gifts, insights, and offers of help.

## STEP FOUR: Be Grateful and Say Thank You

The Past: What have you learned?
Don't take what you have for granted.

The Future: What's next?

Write daily in a gratitude journal.

Today: What will you receive?

Be grateful for something every single day.

## STEP FIVE: Create Full Reciprocity in Your Relationships

The Past: What have you learned?

Trying to fix relationships by giving more leads to your receiving less.

The Future: What's next?

Contribute to relationships by receiving as much as you give.

Today: What will you receive?

Receive your feelings about your relationships.

## STEP SIX: Don't Put Yourself Last or *You* Won't Last

The Past: What have you learned?

You need receptivities in your day to balance and complement your activities.

The Future: What's next?

Make a plan for relaxation.

Today: What will you receive?

Sights, sounds, smells, tastes, and touches.

# Reclaim Your Half of the Universe

Every exercise I have given you and every idea I have presented to you leads you to the doorway of your hopes, desires, and dreams—and then opens the door. That is what receiving does. It draws people to you. It attracts things to you. It opens the world to you.

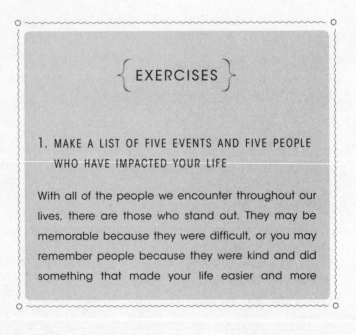

## { EXERCISES }

### 1. MAKE A LIST OF FIVE EVENTS AND FIVE PEOPLE WHO HAVE IMPACTED YOUR LIFE

With all of the people we encounter throughout our lives, there are those who stand out. They may be memorable because they were difficult, or you may remember people because they were kind and did something that made your life easier and more enjoyable. Important events often lead us toward or away from people or places. They determine a large portion of your life. Who are these people and what events helped you become who you are now?

## 2. DON'T TALK ABOUT YOUR SELF-ESTEEM

Don't listen to people who tell you that you need to improve your self-esteem. Some people mean well, but many do not. See them for who they are and what they want. Allow your ideas about yourself to ebb and flow, to rise and fall. Being human and having a variety of feelings about yourself is natural. Spend your time with people who care about you. Don't hang out with people who judge you. Don't read magazines or watch television shows or commercials that tell you something is wrong with you. Instead, do things that you enjoy and that you find meaningful and fulfilling.

## 3. WHAT DO YOU WANT IN YOUR FUTURE?

It's a relief to not have to know how everything will turn out before you do anything. If you are not sure what you want, do the Send Cinderella to Rehab exercise (see page 73). Write in your journal, daydream, take a walk, admire flowers. Something will come to you. When it does, write it down. That is your first step.

## 4. DRAW A BIG CIRCLE AND FILL IT WITH RECEPTIVITIES

What is relaxing for one person may be stressful for someone else. Spend time thinking about what receptivities to include in your Big Circle, and put it where you can see it every day. What receptivities can you do at home? Think of the ones that you can do while you are driving or at work. Feel free to use the Big Circle from this book. But also use your imagination and think about your days, to discover your own.

## 5. CHOOSE THREE TO TEN RECEPTIVITIES FROM YOUR BIG CIRCLE TO DO EVERY DAY

Now that you have your Big Circle with all of those receptivities, choose some of them to do each day. Don't go to sleep at night before doing a minimum of three. Here is an example of receptivities you can easily do during the day:

When you are driving, instead of distracting yourself with phone calls, listening to mindless chatter on the radio, or thinking about where you just left or where you are headed, observe your surroundings. Do you see trees? Do you hear people talking? Is there a rainbow in the distance? Do you smell the exhaust from other cars? How does the steering wheel feel? Are you comfortable? Pay attention.

{ INSPIRING QUOTES }
ABOUT THE PAST,
THE FUTURE,
AND THE PRESENT

*Normal day, let me be aware of the treasure you are.*
*Let me not pass you by in quest of some*
*rare and perfect tomorrow.*

○ MARY JEAN IRION ○

*When busyness is the measure of time, no matter*
*how much time exists it is never enough.*

○ DIANA HUNT ○

*Don't let the past steal your present.*

○ CHERRALEA MORGEN ○

*There are so many ways that have been dreamed*
*up to entertain us away from the moment.*

○ PEMA CHÖDRÖN ○

*The past has helped me appreciate the present and*
*I don't want to spoil it by fretting about the future.*

○ AUDREY HEPBURN ○

> *Creativity exists in the present moment.*
> *You can't find it anywhere else.*
>
> ° NATALIE GOLDBERG °
>
> *The future belongs to those who believe*
> *in the beauty of their dreams.*
>
> ° ELEANOR ROOSEVELT °

# A Summary of the Receive Exercises

**STEP ONE:** Pay Attention to Your
Feelings and Trust Your Intuition

1. Spend Time with Your Feelings

   Write down your feelings about the people you
   know and the places you go.

2. Build and Strengthen Your Feeling
   Receptors

   Choose one feeling and spend the day with it.
   Make a point to notice every time you see that
   feeling expressed, whether in you or in someone
   else.

3. Receive Everything—Decide Later

   Pay attention to your feelings. Don't push them
   away. Receive them. You can decide later about
   what you want to do with what you have received.

## 4. Maintain a Flexible Thermostat

When you want to freak out or shut down, check in with your feelings instead.

## 5. Commit to a Complaint Fast

If you have an impulse to complain, check in with your feelings instead. Sit with them a bit. Become familiar with what they are telling you.

### STEP TWO: Know What You Want

## 1. Don't Obsess about What You *Don't* Want

When you find yourself thinking about what you *don't* want, replace those thoughts with what you *do* want. Give yourself something to aim for.

## 2. Send Cinderella to Rehab

Find a quiet place where you can be alone. Fill three pages writing what you want. *I want* [fill in the blank], *I want* [fill in the blank], *I want* [fill in the blank].

## 3. Choose What You Want

Be specific. Once you know what you want, you will be able to ask for it.

### 4. Say What You Want

Let people know what you want. Don't ask only for those things that you think others will agree with. Ask for exactly what you want.

### 5. Write Down What You Want

Start with one goal and give it your undivided attention. Give it a completion date so that you can evaluate whether or not you have reached your goal.

## STEP THREE: Ask for Help When You Need It and Accept It When It's Offered

### 1. "Ask a Mortal Day"

Designate one day each week to ask people for help, whether you need someone to help you sort through a problem, need help finding a job, or would love to learn a new recipe.

### 2. Notice and Acknowledge the People Who Help You Every Day

Don't spend your days on autopilot. Who is performing tasks for you? Notice them. Say something. Smile!

### 3. Allow People to Reciprocate

If you do something for someone and they want to return the favor, let them.

### 4. Make a List of the People from Whom You Would Like Help

Don't try to carry 100 percent of the load. The people in your life are there to help you. Who are they?

### 5. Ask for Exactly What You Need

Don't make people guess. Be specific. If people don't know what you want, how can they give you what you want?

## STEP FOUR: Be Grateful and Say Thank You

### 1. Pay Attention

Be attentive as you move through your day. What do you hear, see, taste, smell, and touch?

### 2. Acknowledge People

Don't treat people you encounter as if they are insignificant. Notice them, talk to them, smile.

### 3. Write in a Gratitude Journal

Each day, write down five things for which are grateful. Choose one and close your eyes. Spend sixty seconds immersing in the memory of that experience.

### 4. Say Thank You

Look for opportunities to thank people. Everywhere you go are people who make your days easier and more enjoyable and help the ones you love. Thank them!

### 5. Give

Who helps you? Who makes your life better? Let them know that you are grateful by doing something for them or giving them something.

## STEP FIVE: Create Full Reciprocity in Your Relationships

### 1. Be a Giver, Not a Doer

Assess your relationships. Are you a giver or a doer? Are the people you know receivers or takers? Are you exhausted by your interactions or are you strengthened by your connections?

### 2. Strengthen Your Receive Muscles

Spend time each day strengthening your receptive powers. Every time you immerse in receptive states, you strengthen your receive muscles.

### 3. Speak Up and Don't Give Up

Give a voice to your ideas, desires, and preferences. Practice! Don't run away from difficult discussions.

## 4. Shed Social Roles

Be authentic and embrace your complexity. Examine your social roles and determine which behaviors feel authentic to you and which ones don't fit the person you are today.

## 5. Create Two-Way-Street Relationships

Do the people you care about, care as much about you? How do they show it? Do you need to cut anyone loose? Whom do you want to spend more time with?

## STEP SIX: Don't Put Yourself Last or *You* Won't Last

## 1. Practice Facing Conflict

Learn to stand your ground and learn to negotiate. Make a point this week to speak up or do what you need to do.

## 2. Balance Activities with Receptivities

Put a list of receptivities where you can see them every day. Check them off after you have done them. At the end of each day, make sure you've done as many receptivities as activities.

### 3. Practice Saying No

Set clear boundaries and hold to them. Don't be so available. Don't be so flexible. Practice saying no without excusing, explaining, or equivocating.

### 4. Don't Give Up

Once you know what you need, don't lose heart, don't let people talk you out of it, don't cave. You know what's fair. You know what's right.

### 5. Come to Your Senses

Choose one of your five senses and enjoy everything you receive through that sense for sixty seconds. Open your receptors and see, hear, taste, smell, touch.

## STEP SEVEN: Be Respectful of Your Past, Have a Vision for Your Future, but Live in the Moment

### 1. Make a List of Five Events and Five People That Have Impacted Your Life

Include both the people and events that made your life easier and you happier, and the ones that made your life difficult and added to your struggles. How did they help you become who you are today?

## 2. Don't Talk about Your Self-Esteem

Don't listen to people who tell you that you need to improve your self-esteem. Don't read magazines or watch television shows or commercials that tell you something is wrong with you. Instead, do things that you enjoy and that you find meaningful and fulfilling.

## 3. What Do You Want in Your Future?

It's a relief to not have to know how everything will turn out before you do anything. Write in your journal, daydream, take a walk, admire flowers. Something will come to you. When it does, write it down.

## 4. Draw a Big Circle and Fill It with Receptivities

Spend time thinking about what receptivities to include in your Big Circle. Use your imagination. What receptivities can you do at home? Think of the ones that you can do while you are driving or at work.

## 5. Choose Three to Ten Receptivities from Your Big Circle to Do Every Day

Pay attention throughout your day and be on the lookout for places and times to do your receptivities. Don't go to sleep at night before doing a minimum of three receptivities.

# A List of Receptivities

Add you own receptivities to this list. Be creative. What is relaxing to some people is stressful for others.

Read a book, newspaper, magazine, article.

Play solitaire with cards or on your computer.

Rest.

Sleep.

Soak in a bathtub.

Meditate.

Do yoga, tai chi, or qigong.

Listen to music.

Spend time in nature.

Pet your cat or dog.

Watch birds.

Write in a gratitude journal.

Putter.

Doodle.

Look at water: the ocean, river, lake, or a pond.

Admire flowers.

Draw.

Paint.

Sculpt.

Garden.

Do a guided imagery exercise.

Practice Pranayama (yogic deep breathing).

Get a massage.

Practice biofeedback.

Cook.

Lie on the beach.

Hold hands.

Brush your hair.

Taste delicious food.

Use aromatherapy.

Look at the stars.

Watch clouds.

Sit in the sun.

Be grateful.

Daydream.

Rest.

Engage in hobbies.

Watch comedy.

Knit.

Sew.

Quilt.

Craft.

Enjoy a cup of tea.

Watch nature scenes on your computer, tablet, or phone.

Listen to the sounds of nature on your computer, tablet, or phone.

Go for a walk.

Watch whales.

Crochet.

Take a nap.

Feed ducks.

Sit quietly and listen
to the sounds in your
environment.

Smell flowers.

Have your back
scratched.

Hug someone
you love.

Count sheep.

Watch a movie.

# Acknowledgments

Writing is a solitary act. Creating a book isn't. I am grateful to so many people whose generosity and hard work made it possible for me to bring *Born to Receive* to you.

I'd first like to thank my agent, Bob Silverstein, for his unwavering support and his faith in me and my message. Special thanks to my publisher, Joel Fotinos, for giving me the opportunity to write a second book for Tarcher/Penguin. Every writer should be this lucky. Thanks also to my editor, Andrew Yackira, for his keen editorial eye, and to copy editor Dorian Hastings for her excellent catches and questions.

I owe a debt of gratitude to Kathy Papajohn for her editorial help. Her expertise, along with her enthusiasm for *Born to Receive*, kept me going when I questioned my ability to write a coherent sentence, let alone a book. I am especially grateful to Judi Bagnato for her help with the manuscript. I benefitted immensely from her careful attention and helpful feedback. She helped me transfer my vision for *Born to Receive* onto the page and always pushed me to dig deeper and reach higher. Many thanks also to Jeanne Lombardo for her valuable insights and excellent suggestions.

I am very grateful to the following people for their support, contributions, and input: Rochelle L'Italien, Mingo Stroeber, Kathleen Malone, Maria DeSimone, Anne Stokes Hochberg, Donna Cunningham, Dawn Budetto, Esther Ramos, Judy Brotman, Cheryl Maloney, Liz Lyons, Mary DiGiulian, Janey McCarthy, Shiang Chen-Williams, and Pedro Pablo Sacristán Sanz. Thanks to Bonnie Swanson for the phrase: "We are taught to over-achieve and under-receive."

Finally, I'd like to thank Patricia Sinclair for her generosity and for giving me the perfect environment in which to write.

# Resources for Additional Support and Inspiration

## Books

Abram, David. *The Spell of the Sensuous: Perception and Language in a More-Than-Human World*. New York: Vintage Books, 1997.

Ackerman, Diane. *A Natural History of the Senses*. New York: Vintage Books, 1991.

Ban Breathnach, Sarah. *Simple Abundance: A Daybook of Comfort and Joy*. New York: Grand Central, 2009.

Beattie, Melody. *The New Codependency: Help and Guidance for Today's Generation*. New York: Simon & Schuster Paperbacks, 2009.

Bloom, Lisa. *Think: Straight Talk for Women to Stay Smart in a Dumbed-Down World*. New York: Vanguard Press, 2011.

Boorstein, Sylvia. *Pay Attention, for Goodness' Sake: The Buddhist Path of Kindness*. New York: Ballantine Books, 2003.

Borysenko, Joan. *Fried: Why You Burn Out and How to Revive*. Carlsbad, Calif.: Hay House, Inc., 2011.

Chödrön, Pema. *Living Beautifully: With Uncertainty and Change*. Boston, Mass.: Shambhala, 2012.

Coleman, Penny. *Adventurous Women: Eight True Stories about Women Who Made a Difference*. New York: Henry Holt and Co., 2006.

_____. *Elizabeth Cady Stanton and Susan B. Anthony: A Friendship that Changed the World*. New York: Henry Holt, 2011.

Collins, Gail. *America's Women: 400 Years of Dolls, Drudges, Helpmates, and Heroines*. New York: William Morrow Paperbacks, 2007.

_____. *When Everything Changed: The Amazing Journey of American Women from 1960 to the Present*. New York: Little, Brown, 2009.

De Becker, Gavin. *The Gift of Fear and Other Survival Signals that Protect Us from Violence*. New York: Little, Brown, 1997.

Domar, Alice D., and Henry Dreher. *Self-Nurture: Learning to Care for Yourself as Effectively as You Care for Everyone Else*. New York: Viking, 2000.

Feldt, Gloria. *No Excuses: 9 Ways Women Can Change How We Think about Power*. Berkeley, Calif.: Seal Press, 2010.

Frankel, Louis P. *Nice Girls Just Don't Get It*. New York: Crown Publishers, 2011.

Gbowee, Leymah, and Carol Mithers. *Mighty Be Our Powers: How Sisterhood, Prayer, and Sex Changed a Nation at War*. New York: Beast Books, 2011.

Hay, Louise L. *Empowering Women: Every Woman's Guide to Successful Living*. 17th ed. Carlsbad, Calif.: Hay House, 1999.

————. *Gratitude: A Way of Life*. Carlsbad, Calif.: Hay House, 1996.

Herz, Rachel. *The Scent of Desire: Discovering Our Enigmatic Sense of Smell*. New York: William Morrow, 2007.

Horowitz, Alexandra. *On Looking: Eleven Walks with Expert Eyes*. New York: Scribner, 2013.

Ledbetter, Lilly, and Lanier Scott Isom. *Grace and Grit: My Fight for Equal Pay and Fairness at Goodyear and Beyond*. New York: Crown Archetype, 2012.

Lerner, Gerda. *Fireweed: A Political Autobiography*. Philadelphia, Pa.: Temple University Press, 2002.

Lesser. Elizabeth. *The Seeker's Guide: Making Your Life a Spiritual Adventure*. New York: Villard, 2000.

Northrup, M.D., Christiane. *Women's Bodies, Women's Wisdom: Creating Physical and Emotional Health and Healing*. Rev. ed. New York: Bantam Books, 2010.

Owen, Amanda. *The Power of Receiving: A Revolutionary Approach to Giving Yourself the Life You Want and Deserve*. New York: Jeremy. P. Tarcher/Penguin, 2010.

Real, Terrence. *How Can I Get Through to You?: Closing the Intimacy Gap Between Men and Women.* New York: Scribner, 2003.

Rosenberg, Marshall B. *Nonviolent Communication: A Language of Life.* Encinitas, Calif.: PuddleDancer Press, 2003.

Rosenthal, M.D., Norman E. *The Emotional Revolution: Harnessing the Power of Your Emotions for a More Positive Life.* New York: Citadel Press Books, 2003.

Singer, Michael A. *The Untethered Soul: The Journey beyond Yourself.* Oakland, Calif.: New Harbinger Publications and Noetic Books, 2007.

Thich Nhat Hanh. *The Miracle of Mindfulness: An Introduction to the Practice of Meditation.* Boston, Mass.: Beacon Press, 1999.

_____. *You Are Here: Discovering the Magic of the Present Moment.* Boston, Mass.: Shambhala Library 2012.

## Journal

Owen, Amanda. *The Power of Receiving Journal.* Available online at www.AmandaOwen.com.

## Website

www.AmandaOwen.com

If you enjoyed this book, visit

**www.tarcherbooks.com**

and sign up for Tarcher's e-newsletter to receive
special offers, giveaway promotions, and
information on hot upcoming releases.

**TARCHER
PENGUIN**

*Great Lives Begin with Great Ideas*

**Connect with the Tarcher Community**

• • •

Stay in touch with favorite authors!
Enter weekly contests!
Read exclusive excerpts!
Voice your opinions!

**Follow us**

 Tarcher Books

@TarcherBooks

If you would like to place a bulk order
of this book, call 1-800-847-5515.